CORPORATE FINANCE AND CAPITAL STRUCTURE

Capital structure choice is essential for an institution to maximize its value. Because the institution's decision maker decides how to finance projects before making investment decisions, its financial decisions ultimately affect every aspect of operations thereafter. This book discusses several key theories of corporate capital structure to answer how funding structure shapes an institution's value.

In this book, the author emphasizes the microeconomic foundations of capital structure theory. He shows how various microeconomic frameworks, such as price and game theories, principal–agent model, and mechanism design, can be applied to solve the optimal capital structure of a firm. By getting used to optimizing corporate capital structures subject to various constraints via microeconomic frameworks, readers will become capable of investigating how to finance projects in their own setups. Thus, this book not only informs readers of specific knowledge but also provides them with tools to solve new problems that they will face in their future.

This book will be a valuable resource for students of corporate finance at the postgraduate or doctoral level and will serve as the material for professional training aimed at practitioners and regulators with technical expertise.

Kentaro Asai joined Australian National University in 2016 as an assistant professor in the College of Business and Economics. He earned his PhD, MA, and BA with Honors in economics from the University of Chicago. He has published internationally in scholarly journals and policy reports in economics and finance. He is also a former security analyst at Goldman Sachs.

CORPORATE FINANCE AND CAPITAL STRUCTURE

A Theoretical Introduction

Kentaro Asai

LONDON AND NEW YORK

First published 2021
by Routledge
2 Park Square, Milton Park, Abingdon, Oxon OX14 4RN

and by Routledge
52 Vanderbilt Avenue, New York, NY 10017

Routledge is an imprint of the Taylor & Francis Group, an informa business

British Library Cataloguing-in-Publication Data
A catalogue record for this book is available from the British Library

Library of Congress Cataloging-in-Publication Data
Names: Asai, Kentaro, author.
Title: Corporate finance and capital structure : a theoretical introduction / Kentaro Asai.
Description: Abingdon, Oxon ; New York, NY : Routledge, 2021. |
    Includes bibliographical references and index.
Identifiers: LCCN 2020035545 (print) | LCCN 2020035546 (ebook) |
    ISBN 9780367860066 (paperback) | ISBN 9780367860059 (hardback) |
    ISBN 9781003016380 (ebook)
Subjects: LCSH: Corporations—Finance. | Capital. | Valuation.
Classification: LCC HG4026 .A835 2021 (print) | LCC HG4026 (ebook) |
    DDC 658.15/2—dc23
LC record available at https://lccn.loc.gov/2020035545
LC ebook record available at https://lccn.loc.gov/2020035546

ISBN: 978-0-367-86005-9 (hbk)
ISBN: 978-0-367-86006-6 (pbk)
ISBN: 978-1-003-01638-0 (ebk)

Typeset in Times New Roman
by Apex CoVantage, LLC

CONTENTS

CONTENTS

1

INTRODUCTION

1.1 What this book is about

Capital structure is a key determinant of a firm's value. Because the firm's decision maker decides how to finance projects before making investment decisions, her financial decisions ultimately affect every aspect of operations thereafter. For example, the funding structure of the firm affects the amount of tax payment, managerial incentives for investing efficiently, and the perception of external investors toward the institution. The natural questions include the following: How does the firm's funding structure affect its value?; How does the firm's decision maker choose its capital structure?; and What capital structure maximizes firm value?

These questions matter not only to firms but also to households and individuals as well. When you build up houses, should you use mortgage loans or your own money? When you plan to go to college, should you use student loans or equity-like scholarships as in Australia? These questions are ubiquitous in our lives. Although this book focuses on corporate capital structure, its implication is widely applicable to our financial decisions.

To answer them, this book discusses several key theories of corporate capital structure. It starts by proposing capital structure is neutral to firm value in a frictionless capital market. Then, it progresses to consider how frictions and institutions alter the capital structure of a firm. As the first attempt to deviate from a frictionless world, I study the choice of capital structure in the presence of corporate tax and default, that is, the so-called trade-off theory. I then briefly survey the empirical relevance of this theory. Finding some evidence that is inconsistent with this theory, I introduce alternative theories of capital structure. For example, I study the capital structure of a firm when a firm's decision maker's incentives deviate from maximizing the value of a firm. I also investigate the payoff schedule of a financial contract in the presence of hidden actions, limited liability, costly state verification, and contract incompleteness. In addition, I consider information asymmetry between an entrepreneur and an investor, allowing us to interpret capital structure as a signaling device that affects the value of a firm. This idea progresses to the so-called pecking-order theory. I discuss the empirical relevance of this theory in comparison to trade-off theory. I then address how stylistic models can be converted to structural models that can yield quantitative implications. Besides corporate capital structure, I also discuss the capital structure of a bank. In particular, I cover a bank run, deposit insurance, moral hazard in the presence of deposit insurance, and capital regulation that mitigates the moral hazard problem.

1.2 Chapter overview

I summarize the chapter progression as follows.

Chapter 2

I start by introducing the Arrow–Debreu model and proving the unique existence of equilibrium state prices in a frictionless capital market. Then, I show the choice of financing instruments is neutral to the maximization of firm value in the economy. The chapter is used to establish the benchmark result for the capital structure of a firm. Knowing this result, readers can understand the roles of various frictions and institutions in the choice of capital structure that are later discussed.

Chapter 3

I introduce the tax benefit of debt and the cost of financial distress owing to a firm's default (trade-off theory). Then, I show trading off the two factors through debt issuance affects firm value and solve the optimal debt level that maximizes firm value. I then discuss the empirical relevance of the hypothesis that such the optimal debt level matches the actual choice of capital structure. In particular, I show some inconsistencies with observed data to motivate alternative theories for a firm's capital structure.

Chapter 4

I cover the agency model to examine how capital structure affects a controlling owner's investment incentives. The model shows that external equity finance distorts a controlling owner's investment incentives whereas default-free debt is neutral to her incentives. This result suggests that external equity finance can reduce firm value through inefficient investment or, in other words, induce agency cost. I also show the use of debt can induce agency cost if debt is risky. In particular, I show that it can distort the controlling owner's investment incentives through debt overhang (underinvestment) and risk shifting (excessive investment). Overall, this chapter discusses the alternative benefit and cost of debt from the perspective of agency problem.

Chapter 5

I derive the optimal payoff schedule of a financial contract in various settings utilizing contract theory. Then, I show the derived contract resembles debt. Through this analysis, I discuss the benefit of using debt from the perspective of security design.

Chapter 6

I introduce information asymmetry between firms and investors in the capital market. I start by showing that investors require discounts on the prices of a firm's issuing securities when they do not know which firm is good and which is not, motivating the need for signaling the firm's type. Then, I investigate how firms can signal their types through their capital structure choice. I first show an entrepreneur can signal its better quality by retaining ownership.

I second show she can also signal its better quality by raising debt. These findings suggest that the natural priority of financing instruments. She first uses internal capital, then raises debt, and raises equity as a "last resort" (pecking-order theory). I discuss the empirical relevance of this theory in comparison to trade-off theory.

Chapter 7

In this chapter, I demonstrate how stylistic models can be converted to structural models that can yield quantitative implications. I present two continuous-time models that correspond to the one covered by Chapter 2 in which capital structure choice is neutral to firm value and the trade-off theory covered by Chapter 3 in which the firm optimally trades off the tax benefit of debt and the cost of financial distress, respectively.

Chapter 8

In this chapter, I discuss the capital structure of a bank. I commence by showing that coordination failure among creditors can cause a bank run and that deposit insurance can eliminate the possibility of a bank run. I, however, argue deposit insurance can cause excessive risk-taking, requiring a regulation that mitigates this problem. I then show modulating the funding structure of a bank through capital regulation can mitigate a bank's excessive risk-taking. I thus address the regulatory importance of capital structure in the banking sector.

Although I focus on capital structure in this book, the ideas and frameworks covered in these chapters are recurrent and reusable in any corporate finance topic. By getting used to the analysis of corporate capital structure subject to various constraints with microeconomic tools, readers become capable of investigating their own research questions in corporate finance. Thus, this book not only informs readers of specific knowledge but also provides them with tools to solve new problems that they will face in their future.

2

CAPITAL STRUCTURE CHOICE IN A
FRICTIONLESS WORLD

2.1 Overview

In the simplest form of capital structure theory, a firm is a mere machine that generates cash flows automatically. Then, a firm's capital structure choice is a mere choice of how to divide up cash flows across claim holders. In a frictionless world, security valuation becomes additive and unique. Therefore, the sum of prices paid into a firm is identical regardless of how cash flows are divided up among claim holders. In this chapter, we clarify the conditions for a capital market to be frictionless under which capital structure is irrelevant to firm value.

2.2 Frictionless capital market

Whereas being frictionless could mean a lot in potential, Modigliani and Miller (1958) focused on the *absence of arbitrage opportunities* and the presence of *market completeness*. How do these two conditions exactly play in a capital market? To answer this question, I review the Arrow–Debreu model of security pricing.

Although Arrow and Debreu (1954) generalized it to the economy with arbitrary dates, it suffices to analyze the two-dated economy ($t = 0, 1$) for our purpose. There are J non-degenerate states at $t = 1$. A representative agent does not predict actual state realization perfectly, but she knows the probability of state j occurring at $t = 0$, P_j, for $\forall j$. She endogenously chooses investment and consumption decisions at $t = 0$ in the presence of a capital market.

She receives endowments at both periods. At $t = 0$, she receives a fixed endowment X. At $t = 1$, she receives endowment Y_j in state j, defining a vector Y ($J \times 1$). She also has a bundle of N investment opportunities. At $t = 1$, security i pays off Γ_{ij} in state j, defining a payoff matrix Γ ($N \times J$).

I now show how this economy's equilibrium looks. At equilibrium, an agent optimally consumes and invests. Her decision is eventually reduced to her portfolio choice of security i, θ_i, defining a vector θ ($1 \times N$) at $t = 0$. To see how, let V_i be the price of security i, defining a vector V ($N \times 1$). Then, she spends θV for her portfolio at $t = 0$. Assuming a standard utility function $U(C_0, C_1)$, where C_t is consumption at t, she gains by any marginal increase in consumption at each period. She therefore spends all her budgets at both periods. Her budget is $X - \theta V$ at $t = 0$ and $Y + \Gamma' \theta'$ at $t = 1$, taking her endowments into account. Her portfolio choice is characterized by

$$\max_{\theta} E \left[U(X - \theta V, Y + \Gamma' \theta') \right].$$

Here, despite the slight abuse of notation, Y and Γ are considered random variables for the payoffs of the corresponding endowment and securities. The first-order condition with respect to θ_i implies

$$-V_i \sum_{j=1}^{J} P_j U_{0j} + \sum_{j=1}^{J} P_j U_{1j} \Gamma_{ij} = 0,$$

where U_{tj} represents the marginal utility of consumption at t in state j. This condition needs to be satisfied for $\forall i$. It means that the amount of utility lost from the decrease in consumption at $t = 0$ is just equal to the increase in expected utility due to the larger future consumption. Then, the preceding equation is equivalent to

$$V_i = \sum_{j=1}^{J} P_j \Gamma_{ij} \frac{U_{1j}}{\sum_{j=1}^{J} P_j U_{0j}}.$$

In summary, the optimal portfolio choice links the $N \times 1$ vector of securities V to the $N \times J$ matrix of future payoffs by the following relationship:

$$V = \sum_{j=1}^{J} \Gamma_j P_j \frac{U_{1j}}{\sum_{j=1}^{J} P_j U_{0j}},$$

where Γ_j is the $N \times 1$ vector of security payoffs in state j. Recall the expectation is taken over J states, I can rewrite this relation to the following linear relationship:

$$V = \sum_{j=1}^{J} \Gamma_j \psi_j = \Gamma \psi, \qquad (2.1)$$

where $\psi_j = P_j U_{1j} / \sum_{j=1}^{J} P_j U_{0j}$, defining a vector ψ ($J \times 1$). ψ_j is interpreted as the value of one endowment in state j. ψ is often called the state price vector.

Here, I consider an equilibrium exists, or a capital market functions, if agents with *some* standard preference have the finite optima with regard to the previous maximization problem under security prices V and payoff matrix Γ. Indeed, if no agent had the finite optimum under V and Γ, each agent would demand some portfolios infinitely and the capital market would fail. Dybvig and Ross (2003) show the condition for the existence of an equilibrium is equivalent to the existence of a strictly positive state price vector ψ satisfying equation (2.1). Thus, if a capital market functions, security prices must be the product of a payoff matrix and some strictly positive state price vector.

If an equilibrium exists, each security price is *additive* in the sense that it is equal to the sum of value attached to each payoff in each state measured on the common basis, ψ. In other words, it is reducible to a contribution from each payoff in each state.

As discussed by Varian (1987), this result appears obvious at first glance, but it has perhaps surprising implications. To see why, consider the case in which the payoffs of securities A and B are negatively correlated. If two securities with negative correlation are combined, the riskiness of the portfolio will be less than the riskiness of either security held alone. Since the portfolio is less risky than either of the two securities held alone, it might seem that the price of the portfolio would be higher than the sum of the prices of the two securities. However, the price of the portfolio will just be the sum of the prices of the two individual portfolios!

Notice that the equilibrium prices of securities already reflect the possibility of any portfolio manipulation. If the price of the portfolio were above the sum of the prices of the securities alone, then agents could just buy or sell the two securities and countertrade the portfolio to earn sure profits. At equilibrium, such trading is inadmissible, because it makes every agent demand some portfolios without limit.

2.3 Additivity and uniqueness of security valuation

When does an equilibrium exist? To specify the condition of equilibrium existence, I introduce Stiemke's lemma:

- **Stiemke's lemma:** Exactly one of the following two statements is true[1]:

  1 There exists a $\psi \gg 0$ s.t. $V = \Gamma\psi$.
  2 There exists a θ s.t. $\Gamma'\theta \geq 0$ and $\theta V \leq 0$, with at least one strict inequality.

The first case corresponds to the existence of equilibrium. What does the second case mean? If $\theta V \leq 0$ and $\Gamma'\theta \geq 0$ with strict inequality for some θ, an agent is able to weakly increase consumption at $t = 0$ and strictly increase consumption at $t = 1$ by choosing some portfolio. If $\theta V < 0$ and $\Gamma'\theta \geq 0$ for some θ, she is able to strictly increase consumption at $t = 0$ and weakly increase consumption at $t = 1$ by choosing some portfolio. The second case therefore corresponds to the presence of arbitrage opportunities for existing securities in combination. According to this lemma, the absence of arbitrage opportunities for existing securities is equivalent to the existence of equilibrium. Thus, an agent has access to a functioning capital market in which existing securities are priced in an additive manner if and only if there are no arbitrage opportunities between them.

I, however, note I cannot rule out the fickleness of a new security's price entirely even if security pricing is additive and consistent among existing securities. There could be multiple ways of making a new security's price coherent to the prices of existing securities if there are multiple state price vectors such that $V = \Gamma\psi$.

Suppose, for example, there are three securities, A, B, and C, in the capital market where $J = 3$. Security A's payoffs are [1, 0, 0], security B's payoffs are [0, 1, 0], and security C's payoffs are [1, 1, 0]. The payoff matrix of securities is therefore described as

$$\Gamma = \begin{bmatrix} 1 & 0 & 0 \\ 0 & 1 & 0 \\ 1 & 1 & 0 \end{bmatrix}.$$

Let the corresponding security prices be described as

$$V = \begin{bmatrix} 2 \\ 2 \\ 4 \end{bmatrix}.$$

Then for any state price vector,

$$\psi = \begin{bmatrix} 2 \\ 2 \\ v \end{bmatrix},$$

with arbitrary v satisfies $V = \Gamma\psi$. Can I determine the price of a new security D with payoffs [0, 1, 1] in a unique manner? Notice that the payoffs of security D cannot be replicated from any portfolio of existing securities. It is hence impossible to earn sure profits by arbitrating the portfolio of existing securities that replicates the payoffs of security D and countertrading security D itself, meaning multiple prices can be coherent to the prices of existing securities. Indeed, when the price of D is $2 + v$, where v is arbitrary positive number, agents cannot earn sure profits by any transaction.

In fact, market completeness eliminates this indeterminacy. Here, a complete market means the presence of J independent existing securities. Securities are independent if their payoff vectors are linearly independent. On the other hand, if a security, say l, has a payoff that can be replicated using a linear combination of other security payoffs, then l is said to be redundant. Notice there are at most J independent securities. To see how, suppose there are two independent securities, where $J = 2$ with payoff vectors (1, 0) and (0, 1). Then, an arbitrary payoff vector (a, b) is representable as a linear combination of (1, 0) and (0, 1) as $(a, b) = a(1, 0) + b(0, 1)$. Indeed, any payoff vector can be replicated by the linear combination of J independent securities in this economy. By definition, the presence of J independent existing securities is equivalent to the full rankness of Γ. Because a unique solution exists for $V = \Gamma\psi$ for Γ that is full rank, a *unique* equilibrium exists in the absence of arbitrage opportunities and the presence of market completeness. Then, when a new security is born, it needs to be evaluated based on the unique state price vector.

To see how, consider the previous example where security C is replaced by security C' whose payoffs are [1, 0, 1]. Whereas the payoffs of security C are linearly dependent on the payoffs of securities B and C, the payoffs of security C' are linearly independent of them. Then

$$\Gamma = \begin{bmatrix} 1 & 0 & 0 \\ 0 & 1 & 0 \\ 1 & 0 & 1 \end{bmatrix},$$

which is full rank. Assuming the same V, the unique state price vector,

$$\psi = \begin{bmatrix} 2 \\ 2 \\ 2 \end{bmatrix},$$

exists such that $V = \Gamma\psi$. Because Γ is full rank now, ψ is uniquely determined. Can I determine the price a new security D with payoffs [0, 1, 1] in a unique manner? Notice the payoffs of security D can be now replicated by buying one unit of securities B and C' each and selling one unit of security A. The price of this portfolio is 4 (2 + 4 − 2). If

7

the price of security D is not equal to 4, it is possible to earn sure profits by arbitrating this portfolio and security D. Thus, the price of security D is uniquely determined to the price of this portfolio, which is equal to $[0, 1, 1]\psi$.

In summary, any security is priced in an additive and unique manner in the absence of arbitrage opportunities and the presence of market completeness.

• **Additivity and uniqueness of security pricing:** Suppose the economy in the absence of arbitrage opportunities and the presence of market completeness. Then, the price of a security with a payoff Z is $Z\psi$, where ψ is the unique state price vector.

2.4 Neutrality of capital structure

Modigliani and Miller (1958) showed the irrelevance of corporate capital structure in the presence of a complete market without arbitrage opportunities. To acquire this result, they omitted many institutions observed in practice, such as corporate tax, bankruptcy cost, and asymmetric information between firms and agents. In addition, they assumed exogenous cash flows generated by a firm. With these assumptions, they established the benchmark condition in which a firm's role was minimized to a mere generator of stochastic payoffs like one of the securities in the economy. Any claim on a firm's payoffs was then also considered one of the securities in the economy. By interpreting the values of firm, debt, and equity as the prices of securities in the economy, they utilized the implications from the Arrow–Debreu model.[2]

Let me show the irrelevance of corporate capital structure in the context of the Arrow–Debreu model. At $t = 0$, a firm attempts to raise funds for a project that matures at $t = 1$. A firm's project yields cash flows Z_j in state j at $t = 1$, defining a vector Z $(1 \times J)$. There are two ways to finance this project (1) equity only and (2) equity and debt. When debt is issued, a firm is said to be levered. Otherwise, it is called unlevered. A firm's investor has limited liability.

If a firm is unlevered, it issues only equity whose payoff is Z. Limited liability ensures shareholders' claims are nonnegative. Then the payoff of the unlevered firm's equity is $[Z]^+$, where the jth element of $[Z]^+$, is $\max\{Z_j, 0\}$. In the presence of market completeness and the absence of arbitrage opportunities between existing securities, the additivity and uniqueness of security pricing suggest that the price of equity for the unlevered firm V_U satisfies

$$V_U = [Z]^+ \, \psi, \tag{2.2}$$

where ψ is the unique state price vector in the economy.

If a firm is levered, then it issues both equity and debt. Let me assume the face value of debt is F $(F > 0)$. At $t = 1$, if $F > Z_j$, a firm goes bankrupt and debt holders receive $\max\{Z_j, 0\}$, meaning that bankruptcy is defined as the set of states where a firm is unable to pay its debt. Then the payoff of debt in the jth state is $B_j = \min\{F, \max\{Z_j, 0\}\}$, defining a vector B $(1 \times J)$. Equity holders have a residual claim while being protected by limited liability. Then the payoff of equity in the jth state is $S_j = \max\{Z_j - \min\{F, \max\{Z_j, 0\}\}, 0\} = \max\{Z_j, 0\} - \min\{F, \max\{Z_j, 0\}\}$, defining a vector S $(1 \times J)$. In the presence of market completeness and the absence of arbitrage opportunities between existing securities, the additivity and uniqueness of security pricing suggest that the price of debt is $B\psi$ whereas the price of equity is $S\psi$. By definition, the value of the levered firm V_L is the sum of the prices of these two securities:

$$V_L = B\psi + S\psi. \tag{2.3}$$

Because $B_j + S_j = \max\{Z_j, 0\}$ for $\forall j$, $B + S = [Z]^+$, owing to the additivity of security pricing, $B\psi + S\psi = (B + S)\psi = [Z]^+\psi$, suggesting that

$$V_U = V_L. \tag{2.4}$$

Then, I claim the follwing:

- **Irrelevance of capital structure:** Suppose the economy in the absence of arbitrage opportunities and the presence of market completeness. Then, the values of unlevered and levered firms that generate the same cash flows are identical.

The preceding claim is natural if security pricing is additive because, regardless of how you divide up payoffs, the price of aggregate payoffs is unaltered. In Figure 2.1, I compare the payoff schedule of unlevered equity, debt, and equity. The top panel shows the payoff schedule of unlevered equity. The bottom panel shows the payoff schedules of debt and equity for a corresponding levered firm. As you see, the payoff schedule of unlevered equity for an unlevered firm is the sum of debt and equity for a corresponding levered firm. Under additive security pricing, the sum of debt and equity prices should match the price of unlevered equity. For this reason, assuming the absence of arbitrage opportunities is necessary for deriving the irrelevance of capital structure

The implication of market completeness and unique security pricing might not be obvious at the first glance. To see it, suppose, for example, there are three securities A, B, and C in the capital market where $J = 3$. Security A's payoffs are $[1, 0, 0]$, security B's payoffs are $[0, 1, 0]$, and security C's payoffs are $[1, 1, 0]$ as in one of the examples earlier. Now, consider a *single* firm that generates payoffs $[1, 1, 0.5]$ enters the economy. First, I consider a case where the firm issues unlevered equity. Then, agents cannot make sure profits when the price of unlevered equity is $4 + 0.5v_1$, where v_1 is an arbitrary positive value. Second, I consider a case in which the firm issues both debt with a face value 0.7 and equity. The debt payoffs are $[0.7, 0.7, 0.5]$ whereas the equity payoffs are $[0.3, 0.3, 0]$. Then, agents cannot earn sure profits when the price of debt is $2.8 + 0.5v_2$, where v_2 is arbitrary positive value. The price of equity has to be 1.2—otherwise, agents could arbitrate this security and the portfolio consisting of securities A and B. The value of the levered firm is hence $4 + 0.5v_2$. Then, if $v_1 \neq v_2$, $V_U \neq V_L$, suggesting that the value of a levered firm is not same as the value of an unlevered firm. Thus, if a market is incomplete, the values of levered and unlevered firms may not match.

However, assuming market completeness may not be essential for the irrelevance of capital structure under certain circumstances. For example, suppose *multiple* firms that generate the same payoffs enter the economy. Each firm generates payoffs, $[1, 1, 0.5]$. One firm is unlevered and the other is levered. The levered firm's capital structure is the same as the one in the previous paragraph. According to the argument in the previous paragraph, the price of the unlevered firm's equity needs to be $4 + 0.5v_1$ and the price of the portfolio that replicates the levered firm's payoffs needs to be $4 + 0.5v_2$, where v_1 and v_2 are arbitrary

(a) Unlevered Firm

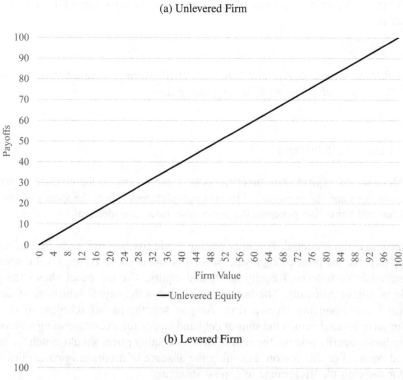

(b) Levered Firm

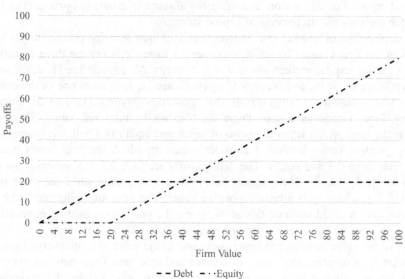

Figure 2.1 Payoffs of Securities

positive values, so that agents cannot earn sure profits by countertrading *each for any port-folio of existing securities*. Notice, however, agents can also countertrade *each for the other* when both firms are present. To prohibit agents from earning sure profits, $v_1 = v_2 = v$ holds, where v is arbitrary positive value. If $v_1 = v_2$, $V_U = V_L$, the value of the levered firm is the same as the value of the unlevered firm. Thus, the capital structure may not affect the firm's value even if a market is incomplete and multiple equilibria exist.

2.5 Discussion

In this chapter, I derive the irrelevance of capital structure based on Modigliani and Miller (1958). Although it is tempting to apply their implication directly to the real economy, researchers rather appreciate their work for showing us how much simplication is required to achieve the neutrality of capital structure. First, additive and unique security valuation requires the presence of a complete market and the absence of arbitrage opportunities among existing securities. Second, as assumed by Modigliani and Miller (1958), many institutions observed in practice, such as corporate tax, bankruptcy cost, and asymmetric information between firms and agents, need to be excluded from the economy. Third, a firm has to be a mere generator of payoffs. These assumptions make the economy simple enough to achieve the neutrality of capital structure.

For the following chapters, I relax these assumptions to generate a situation in which the capital structure is no longer neutral. For example, in the next chapter, I introduce corporate tax and bankruptcy cost that generate the value and cost of levering a firm. In Chapter 4, I consider the condition under which a firm's cash flows are generated from a firm's decision maker who may not have an incentive to maximize firm value. Under that situation, the choice of debt and equity financing matters to the decision maker's actions and the firm's value subsequently.

Notes

1 Whereas $a \gg b$ means that every element of a is strictly greater than b, $a \geq b$ ($a \leq b$) means that every element of a is at least (most) b.
2 In fact, Modigliani and Miller (1958) proved this claim in the slightly different but similar context of the Arrow–Debreu model. Hirshleifer (1966) explicitly used the argument of the Arrow–Debreu model to prove this claim.

Bibliography

Arrow, K. J. and Debreu, G. (1954). Existence of an equilibrium for a competitive economy. *Econometrica*, 22(3):265–90.

Dybvig, P. H. and Ross, S. A. (2003). Arbitrage, state prices and portfolio theory. In Constantinides, G., Harris, M., and Stulz, R., editors, *Financial Markets and Asset Pricing, Volume 1 of Handbook of the Economics of Finance*, Chapter 10, pages 605–37. Elsevier, Amsterdam.

Hirshleifer, J. (1966). Investment decision under uncertainty: Applications of the state-preference approach. *Quarterly Journal of Economics*, 80(2):252–77.

Modigliani, F. and Miller, M. (1958). The cost of capital, corporation finance and the theory of investment. *American Economic Review*, 48(3):261–97.

Varian, H. R. (1987). The arbitrage principle in financial economics. *Economic Perspectives*, 1(2):55–72.

3

TRADE-OFF THEORY

3.1 Criticism against Modigliani and Miller

One of the key assumptions behind the neutrality of capital structure proposed by Modigliani and Miller (1958) is a tax-free environment. In reality, corporate income tax exists and generates the *tax benefit of debt* (tax shield) because interest expenses are tax-deductible. They admitted their unrealistic assumption and later introduced the impact of corporate income tax on corporate capital structure in Modigliani and Miller (1963). Furthermore, Miller wanted to include not only corporate income tax but also personal income taxes into the theory of corporate capital structure. Specifically, Miller (1977) considered different personal tax rates paid by holders of shares and debts. The criticism raised by these papers is relevant, but it also creates a new problem—it suggests the near exclusion of equity financing. What factor prevents the firm from raising debt infinitely?

The other assumption behind the neutrality of capital structure is the absence of *bankruptcy costs*. When a firm defaults, the firm's stakeholders usually incur deadweight loss, because buyers of liquidated assets cannot manage them as efficiently as the failing firm's manager. A number of authors (e.g., Baxter, 1967), since the publication of Modigliani and Miller (1958), suggested that bankruptcy costs could rationalize the existence of a finite debt–equity ratio. Scott (1976) formally introduced bankruptcy costs in their models.

Combining both arguments, financiers have claimed that an optimal, finite debt-equity ratio can exist, resulting from a trade-off between the expected value of bankruptcy costs and the tax savings associated with the deductibility of interest payments (Haugen and Senbet, 1978). Figure 3.1 shows how the optimal level of debt is determined. In the next section, I cover the canonical model by Bradley et al. (1984) to see how this "trade-off" theory works.[1]

3.2 Tax benefit of debt and bankruptcy costs

The model is static. The investors are risk-neutral, and their interest income is subject to a tax rate τ_{pb} ($0 \leq \tau_{pb} \leq 1$). A tax rate τ_{ps} is imposed on their income from dividends and capital gains ($0 \leq \tau_{ps} \leq 1$). A firm's end-of-period wealth X is subject to a constant marginal tax rate τ_c as long as the firm does not default ($X \geq 0$, $0 \leq \tau_c \leq 1$). If the firm defaults, it is not subject to corporate income tax. Its probability density function (PDF) is $f(X)$ and its cumulative distribution function (CDF) is $F(X)$. The firm can deduct both interest and principal payments. The fraction of end-of-period value k is lost at default to capture bankruptcy costs ($0 < k \leq 1$). The risk-free rate is r_f ($r_f \geq 0$). The face value of debt is B, which

12

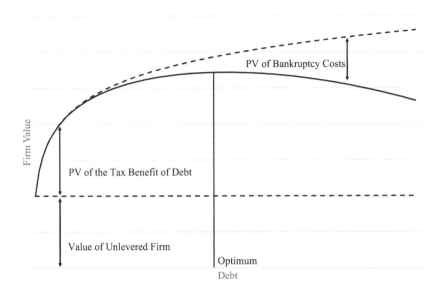

Figure 3.1 Optimal Level of Debt

Table 3.1 Summary of Payoffs

State	Debt	Equity	Tax	Loss
$0 \leq X < B$	$(1-k)X$	0	0	kX
$X \geq B$	B	$(1-\tau_c)(X-B)$	$\tau_c(X-B)$	0

is the single control variable that the firm chooses to maximize firm value ($B \geq 0$). Each stakeholder has limited liability.

When $0 \leq X < B$, the firm defaults and its asset value decreases by kX. The debt holder seizes the firm's asset and receives $(1-k)X$. When $X > B$, the firm survives and the debt holder's payoff is the face value of debt B. The equity holder's payoff is the firm's residual value after a corporate income tax payment $(1-\tau_c)(X-B)$. The tax office's payoff is $\tau_c(X-B)$. The payoff of each stakeholder is summarized in Table 3.1.

Then the market value of debt V_B is the discounted expected payoff of the debt holder after a personal income tax payment as shown:

$$V_B = \frac{1-\tau_{pb}}{1+r_f}\left[\int_B^\infty Bf(X)dX + \int_0^B (1-k)Xf(X)dX\right].$$

Analoguously, the market value of equity V_S is

$$V_S = \frac{1-\tau_{ps}}{1+r_f}\int_B^\infty (1-\tau_c)(X-B)f(X)dX.$$

The firm aims for maximizing the firm's value $V = V_B + V_S$ by optimally choosing B.

One natural question is who determines the size of the debt. If the equity holder or the manager representing the equity holder's interest determines the size of the debt, he or she should maximize V_S. Then, the size of debt becomes zero because V_S monotonically decreases in B. The implicit assumption behind this model is the absence of *agency problem*—the firm's decision maker always maximizes firm value. As you will see in a later chapter, agency problem motivates a different theory of capital structure.

Following the Leibniz rule, the partial derivative of firm value V with respect to B is

$$\frac{\partial V}{\partial B} = \frac{(1 - \tau_{pb})(1 - F(B))}{1 + r_f} \left[\underbrace{\left(1 - \frac{(1 - \tau_c)(1 - \tau_{ps})}{1 - \tau_{pb}} \right)}_{\text{tax benefit of debt}} - \underbrace{kB \frac{f(B)}{1 - F(B)}}_{\text{increase in bankruptcy costs}} \right]. \quad (3.1)$$

The first term inside the bracket of the right-hand side of equation (3.1) captures the marginal tax benefit of debt while the second term is the marginal increase in bankruptcy costs. At the interior optimum, the two terms become equal. Under certain regularity conditions, such interior optimum uniquely exists.

- **Interior optimum:** If $(1 - \tau_c)(1 - \tau_{ps})/(1 - \tau_{pb}) \leq 1$ and F is increasing hazard rate (IHR) distribution function, there is a unique B^* that maximizes firm value V. B^* satisfies $\partial V/\partial B = 0$.

The first term in the bracket is fixed and nonnegative if $(1 - \tau_c)(1 - \tau_{ps})/(1 - \tau_{pb}) \leq 1$, while the second term strictly increases in B, where it is zero when $B = 0$ and diverges to ∞ as $B \to \infty$ if F is IHR distribution function. Then, the first term equals the second term at the unique point. Moreover, a firm can raise value by increasing B ($\partial V/\partial B > 0$) if $B < B^*$, and it can do so by reducing B ($\partial V/\partial B < 0$) if $B > B^*$. Thus, B^* is indeed maximizing firm value.

Next, I investigate comparative statics about the optimal debt level B^*. For an arbitrary parameter p, B^* satisfies $\partial V/\partial B = 0$. Thus, I have

$$\frac{\partial^2 V}{\partial B \partial p}\Big|_{B=B^*} + \underbrace{\frac{\partial^2 V}{\partial B^2}\Big|_{B=B^*}}_{-} \frac{dB^*}{dp} = 0.$$

Recall $\partial V/\partial B > 0$ if $B < B^*$ and $\partial V/\partial B < 0$ if $B > B^*$. $\partial V/\partial B$ decreases in B at B^*. Then, $\partial^2 V/\partial B^2 \leq 0$ at B^*. From the preceding relationship, $dB^*/dp \leq 0$ if $\partial^2 V/\partial B \partial p \leq 0$ at B^* and $dB^*/dp \geq 0$ if $\partial^2 V/\partial B \partial p \geq 0$ at B^*. The effect of a parameter on an endogenous variable depends on the cross partial derivative of an endogenous variable and a parameter. Notice that

$$\frac{\partial^2 V}{\partial B \partial k}\Big|_{B=B^*} = -\frac{(1 - \tau_{pb})B^*}{1 + r_f} f(B^*) \leq 0,$$

$$\frac{\partial^2 V}{\partial B \partial \tau_{ps}}\Big|_{B=B^*} = \frac{(1 - F(B^*))}{1 + r_f} (1 - \tau_c) \geq 0,$$

$$\frac{\partial^2 V}{\partial B \partial \tau_c}\bigg|_{B=B^*} = \frac{(1 - F(B^*))}{1 + r_f}(1 - \tau_{ps}) \geq 0,$$

$$\frac{\partial^2 V}{\partial B \partial \tau_{pb}}\bigg|_{B=B^*} = -\frac{(1 - F(B^*))}{1 + r_f}\frac{(1 - \tau_c)(1 - \tau_{ps})}{(1 - \tau_{pb})} \leq 0.$$

Consequently, I claim the following proposition:

- **Comparative statics:** If $(1 - \tau_c)(1 - \tau_{ps})/(1 - \tau_{pb}) \leq 1$ and F is the IHR distribution function, $dB^*/dk \leq 0$, $dB^*/d\tau_{ps} \geq 0$, $dB^*/d\tau_c \geq 0$, $dB^*/d\tau_{pb} \leq 0$.

If everything else is equal, the net marginal value of an increasing debt level $\partial V/\partial B$ decreases in the level of bankruptcy costs k. It, however, increases in the personal income tax rate on shareholders τ_{ps} and the corporate income tax rate τ_c as both increase the tax benefit of debt. Moreover, it decreases in the personal income tax rate on debt holders τ_{pb}. As a result, the optimal debt level decreases in the level of bankruptcy costs and the personal income tax rate on debt holders, whereas it increases in the personal income tax rate on shareholders, as well as the corporate income tax rate.

3.3 Empirical evidence

Frank and Goyal (2007) provide a comprehensive survey of empirical evidence on capital structure. In this section, I briefly summarize their findings.

First, there have been many empirical papers looking at the relationship between debt and taxes. Taggart (1985) predicts a positive correlation between debt and expected inflation, as the real value of tax deductions on interest payment is higher when inflation is expected to be higher. When the expected inflation rate is higher, the real interest payment needs to increase, because it compensates for the loss in the real value of the principal. The trade-off theory hence suggests a positive correlation between leverage and expected inflation. Consistent with this prediction, Frank and Goyal (2009) show that there is a robust positive correlation between leverage and expected inflation. Moreover, the Undistributed Profits Tax in 1936–7 provides a natural experiment to examine how exogenous tax hikes affect firms' financing decisions. Calomiris and Hubbard (1995) suggest that firms increased their debt after the undistributed profits tax was introduced, which is also consistent with the trade-off theory.

Second, there is the literature that focuses on the empirical relationship between debt and bankruptcy costs. One issue in this literature is how to measure bankruptcy costs from the data set. Some papers, such as Long and Malitz (1985), Barclay et al. (2006), and Frank and Goyal (2009), use a firm's growth opportunities (the ratio of the market value of assets to the book value of assets) as a proxy for bankruptcy costs. The idea is that growing firms lose more of their value when they go bankrupt (higher bankruptcy cost). Another set of papers, such as Frank and Goyal (2009), use asset tangibility (the ratio of tangible assets to total assets) as a proxy, considering firms with collateralizable assets lose less of their value when they go bankrupt (lower bankruptcy cost). The literature has found that the relation between debt and growth is negative whereas the relation between debt and asset tangibility is positive. Both results are consistent with the trade-off theory.

3.4 Discussion

The trade-off theory is one of the earliest models that predicts a firm's capital structure based on realistic assumptions. Indeed, the trade-off theory is fairly consistent with empirical findings. However, it poses some puzzles as well. For example, debt financing was common even before the introduction of the corporate tax system. According to the trade-off theory, a firm never chooses debt in the absence of corporate tax because it only raises bankruptcy costs without any benefits. This observation therefore requires an alternative theory of capital structure. In the next chapter, I introduce an alternative theory of capital structure that focuses on the interaction between how a firm is financed and the incentives of a firm's stakeholders.

Note

1 See also DeAngelo and Masulis (1980) for the model that involves corporate and personal taxes.

Bibliography

Barclay, M. J., Smith, Jr., C. W., and Morellec, E. (2006). On the debt capacity of growth options. *Journal of Business*, 79(1):37–60.

Baxter, N. D. (1967). Leverage, risk of ruin and the cost of capital. *Journal of Finance*, 22(3):395–403.

Bradley, M., Jarrell, G. A., and Kim, E. H. (1984). On the existence of an optimal capital structure: Theory and evidence. *Journal of Finance*, 39(3):857–78.

Calomiris, C. W. and Hubbard, R. G. (1995). Internal finance and investment: Evidence from the undistributed profits tax of 1936–37. *Journal of Business*, 68(4):443–82.

DeAngelo, H. and Masulis, R. W. (1980). Optimal capital structure under corporate and personal taxation. *Journal of Financial Economics*, 8(1):3–29.

Frank, M. Z. and Goyal, V. K. (2007). Trade-off and pecking order theories of debt. In Eckbo, E., editor, *Empirical Corporate Finance, Volume 2 of Handbook of Corporate Finance*, Chapter 12, pages 135–202. Elsevier, Amsterdam.

Frank, M. Z. and Goyal, V. K. (2009). Capital structure decisions: Which factors are reliably important? *Financial Management*, 38(1):1–37.

Haugen, R. A. and Senbet, L. W. (1978). The insignificance of bankruptcy costs to the theory of optimal capital structure. *Journal of Finance*, 33(2):383–93.

Long, M. S. and Malitz, I. B. (1985). Investment patterns and financial leverage. In Friedman, B. M., editor, *Corporate Capital Structures in the United States*, Chapter 9, pages 325–52. University of Chicago Press, Chicago.

Miller, M. H. (1977). Debt and taxes. *Journal of Finance*, 32(2):261–75.

Modigliani, F. and Miller, M. (1958). The cost of capital, corporation finance and the theory of investment. *American Economic Review*, 48(3):261–97.

Modigliani, F. and Miller, M. (1963). Corporate income taxes and the cost of capital: A correction. *American Economic Review*, 53(3):433–43.

Scott, Jr., J. H. (1976). A theory of optimal capital structure. *Bell Journal of Economics*, 7(1):33–54.

Taggart, Jr., R. A. (1985). Secular patterns in the financing of U.S. corporations. In Friedman, B. M., editor, *Corporate Capital Structures in the United States*, Chapter 1, pages 13–80. University of Chicago Press, Chicago.

4

AGENCY THEORY

4.1 Overview

Myers (1977) and Jensen and Meckling (1976) suggest the optimal capital structure minimizes agency problem that arises from stakeholders' incentives deviating from a firm's value maximizer. Unlike the trade-off theory, this theory is consistent with the use of debt prior to the introduction of corporate tax system. A debt contract may or may not give a firm's decision maker an incentive to invest optimally, depending on the possibility of default.

4.2 Safe debt can mitigate agency problem

I begin by showing that safe debt can mitigate agency problem through the two models motivated by Jensen and Meckling (1976).

In the first model, the firm manager invests I and the firm earns $V(I)$ next period, where $V(I)$ satisfies Inada conditions ($I \geq 0$).[1] Under Inada conditions, $V(0) = 0$, $V'(I) > 0$, $V''(I) < 0$, $\lim_{I \to 0} V'(I) = \infty$, $\lim_{I \to \infty} V'(I) = 0$. These conditions are required to induce an interior optimum for the choice of investment I. The risk-free rate is 0.

The manager sells ownership $1 - \alpha$ to finance investment ($0 < \alpha < 1$) and raises E, where $E = (1 - \alpha)V(I)$. If there is a remaining fund, the manager consumes perks. The manager cannot *commit* to her investment decision. This means that she cannot write a contract in a way that she receives E contingent on I. Then, she does not internalize the impact of her investment decision on the amount of funds raised by her E.

First, let us see the socially optimal level of investment I^0, which is the optimal choice of the manager who self-funds investment. Notice the firm value U is such that $U = V(I) - I$. The manager solves the following:

$$\max_{I \geq 0} \ V(I) - I.$$

Then, the first-order condition implies that I^0 satisfies

$$1 = V'(I^0). \tag{4.1}$$

Notice that such an I^0 uniquely exists, because $V'(I)$ strictly decreases in I and ranges from 0 to ∞ for $I \geq 0$. For readers to understand this condition and property, I present Figure 4.1 to visualize equation (4.1).

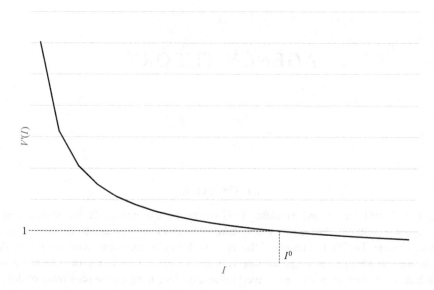

Figure 4.1 Socially Optimal Level of Investment

Second, let us see the equilibrium level of investment I^*. In the presence of external shareholders, the manager maximizes the sum of his portion of investment value and perk consumption subject to the budget constraint:

$$\max_{I \geq 0} \quad \alpha V(I) + E - I,$$

$$\text{s.t.} \quad I \leq E,$$

$$\text{where} \quad E = (1 - \alpha)V(I^*).$$

Then, the first-order condition implies that I^* satisfies

$$\frac{1 + \lambda^*}{\alpha} \quad = \quad V'(I^*), \text{ where } \lambda^* \geq 0. \tag{4.2}$$

Here, λ^* is the Lagrange multiplier associated with the budget constraint.

Given the strict concavity of $V(I)$, $V'(I)$ strictly decreases in I. Because the left-hand side of equation (4.2) exceeds 1, that is, the left-hand side of equation (4.1), $I^* < I^0$. In Figure 4.2, I visualize this result.

Thus, the following claim holds:

- **Underinvestment due to agency problem:** $I^* < I^0$.

The economics behind this result is simple. The manager has to share the net profits of the firm with other shareholders, but she alone consumes the perks. This reduces her incentive to invest relative to a social planner. This problem is called *agency problem*.

18

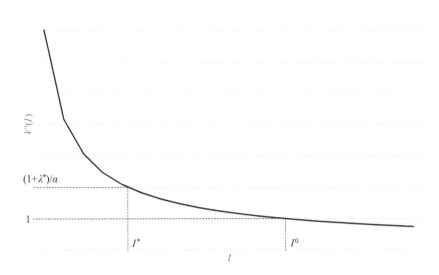

Figure 4.2 Equilibrium Level of Investment

Last, let us see the equilibrium level of investment I^+ when the manager finances investment through debt. Here, debt is *default-free*. Because the risk-free rate is 0, the manager is required to repay only the face value of debt. Let D be the face value of debt. Then, the manager maximizes the sum of his portion of investment value and perk consumption subject to the budget constraint:

$$\max_{I \geq 0} \quad V(I) + D - I - D,$$

$$\text{s.t.} \qquad I \leq D.$$

Then, the first-order condition implies that I^+ satisfies

$$1 + \lambda^+ = V'(I^+), \text{ where } \lambda^+ \geq 0. \tag{4.3}$$

Here, λ^+ is the Lagrange multiplier associated with the budget constraint. In particular, if the manager sufficiently raises debt, the budget constraint never binds. Then, $\lambda^+ = 0$ and equation (4.3) suggests that $I^+ = I^0$, as it completely matches equation (4.1).

- **Optimal investment under debt:** If D is big enough, $I^+ = I^0$.

This result suggests that debt can resolve agency problem by making external finance neutral to an incentive of a firm's decision maker. Thus, there could be an alternative benefit of raising debt other than the tax benefit of debt.

In the second model, the manager chooses effort level e, instead of investment, and the firm earns $V(e)$ in the next period, where $V(e)$ satisfies Inada conditions ($e \geq 0$). As in the previous model, the risk-free rate is 0. The manager sells ownership $1 - \alpha$ to

19

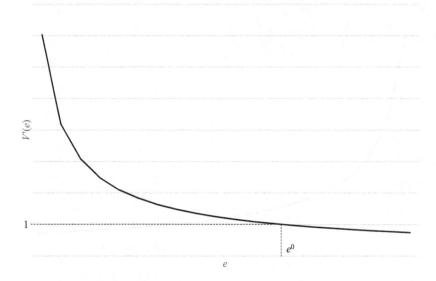

Figure 4.3 Socially Optimal Level of Effort

finance investment ($0 < \alpha < 1$) and raises I, where I is the fixed amount of investment. Here, α is endogenously determined so that the raised fund matches investment demand I. I denote the equilibrium level of α by α^*.

First, let us see the socially optimal level of efforts e^0, which is the optimal choice of the manager who self-funds investment. In this model, firm value U is such that $U = V(e) - e$. The manager solves the following:

$$\max_{e \geq 0} \ V(e) - e.$$

Then the first-order condition implies that e^0 satisfies

$$1 = V'(e^0). \tag{4.4}$$

Such an e^0 uniquely exists as in the previous model. I visualize this result in Figure 4.3. Second, let us see the equilibrium level of efforts e^*. In the presence of external shareholders, the manager solves the following:

$$\max_{e \geq 0} \qquad \alpha^* V(e) - e,$$
$$\text{where} \quad I = (1 - \alpha^*)V(e^*).$$

Then, the first-order condition implies that e^* satisfies

$$\frac{1}{\alpha^*} = V'(e^*). \tag{4.5}$$

Such an e^* uniquely exists given α^* as in the previous model.

20

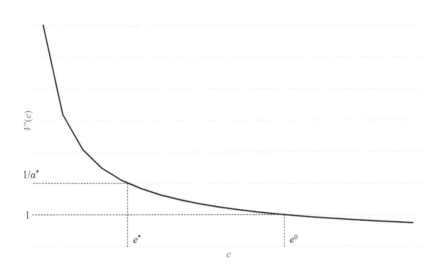

Figure 4.4 Equilibrium Level of Effort

Due to the strict concavity of $V(e)$, $V'(e)$ strictly decreases in e. Because the left-hand side of equation (4.5) exceeds 1, that is, the left-hand side of equation (4.4), $e^* < e^0$. I visualize this result in Figure 4.4.

Thus, the following claim holds:

- **Shirking due to agency problem:** $e^* < e^0$.

The economics behind this result is similar to the one in the previous model. The manager has to share the net profits of the firm with other shareholders, but she alone incurs the cost of making an effort. This reduces her incentive to make an effort relative to a social planner. This problem is also considered *agency problem*.

Last, let us see the equilibrium level of efforts e^+ when the manager finances investment through debt. As in the previous model, debt is *default-free* and its face value is D. Then, the manager solves the following optimization problem:

$$\max_{e \geq 0} \quad V(e) - e - D,$$

$$\text{where} \quad I = D.$$

The first-order condition implies that e^+ satisfies

$$1 = V'(e^+). \tag{4.6}$$

Then, equation (4.6) suggests that $e^+ = e^0$ as it completely matches equation (4.4). The manager optimally makes efforts as in the planner's problem.

- **Optimal efforts under debt:** $e^+ = e^0$.

21

As in the previous model, this result suggests that debt can resolve agency problem by making external finance neutral to an incentive of a firm's decision maker.

4.3 Risky debt can aggravate agency problem

The previous two models suggest that debt finance is superior, given it does not distort a firm's decision maker's incentives. However, they implicitly assume no default. If default is possible, does debt finance minimize agency problem? To answer this question, this section explores a firm's decision maker's incentives when default is possible.

In the next model, motivated by Berkovitch and Kim (1990), the risk-neutral firm has some given assets. There are two equally likely states next period. The risk-free rate is 0. In the high state, the asset value is X_H. In the low state, it is X_L, where $X_H > X_L > 0$. The firm has outstanding debt with a face value F, where $X_H > F > X_L$. If the face value is not repayable, the firm defaults. The firm therefore defaults in the low state as $F > X_L$. When the firm defaults, the owner receives nothing while the debt holder claims the asset. In the low state, the owner hence receives 0 whereas the debt holder receives X_L. In the high state, the owner receives residual claim $X_H - F$ whereas the debt holder receives the face value of debt F. Correspondingly, the expected equity value E_0 satisfies $E_0 = (X_H - F)/2$. The expected debt value D_0 satisfies $D_0 = (F + X_L)/2$. The expected firm value, which is the sum of the expected equity and debt values, V_0 satisfies $V_0 = (X_H + X_L)/2$.

Now, consider the firm has the opportunity of additional investment. The owner determines whether to undertake additional investment and self-finances the project if investing. In particular, there is a safe project I ($I > 0$) with return R regardless of state, where $R > I$ and $0 < X_L + R < F$. The first condition means that the additional investment is profitable for the firm. The second condition means that the firm defaults in the low state. The additional investment increases the payoff of the owner in the high state by R and does not raise his payoff in the low state as the firm defaults. On the other hand, it does not affect the payoff of the debt holder in the high state but raises the payoff in the low state by R. Let E, D, and V be the expected equity, debt, and firm values with additional investment. Then, each value becomes

$$E = (X_H - F + R)/2 - I,$$
$$D = (F + X_L + R)/2,$$
$$V = (X_H + X_L)/2 + R - I.$$

Table 4.1 presents each stakeholder's value with and without additional investment. If $R/2 - I < 0$, $E_0 > E$. Then, the owner does not invest in this project, although the project increases firm value. This outcome is called *debt overhang* (Myers, 1977). This result means that the owner may not invest in a profitable project when the project's return is moderate. This is because the owner cannot acquire all the payoffs from investment as he does not receive any surplus in the low state in which the firm defaults.

If there is no debt, $E = V = (X_H + X_L)/2 + R - I > (X_H + X_L)/2 = V_0 = E_0$. The owner invests in this project and increases firm value unambiguously.

Next, suppose there is a risky project I ($I > 0$) with positive return R_H in the high and R_L in the low state, where $I > (R_H + R_L)/2$ and $0 < X_L + R_L < F$.[2] The first condition means the additional investment is unprofitable for the firm. The second condition means the firm defaults in the low state. The additional investment increases the payoff of the owner in the high state by R_H and does not affect his payoff in the low state as the firm defaults.

Table 4.1 Summary of Payoffs

	Debt	Equity	Unlevered Equity
	With Additional Investment		
High	F	$X_H - F + R - I$	$X_H + R - I$
Low	$X_L + R$	$-I$	$X_L + R-I$
Expectation	$(F + X_L + R)/2$	$(X_H - F + R)/2 - I$	$(X_H + X_L)/2 + R - I$
	Without Additional Investment		
High	F	$X_H - F$	X_H
Low	X_L	0	X_L
Expectation	$(F + X_L)/2$	$(X_H - F)/2$	$(X_H + X_L)/2$

Table 4.2 Summary of Payoffs

	Debt	Equity	Unlevered Equity
	With Additional Investment		
High	F	$X_H - F + R_H - I$	$X_H + R_H - I$
Low	$X_L + R_L$	$-I$	$X_L + R_L - I$
Expectation	$(F + X_L + R_L)/2$	$(X_H - F + R_H)/2-I$	$(X_H + X_L)/2 + (R_H + R_L)/2 - I$
	Without Additional Investment		
High	F	$X_H - F$	X_H
Low	X_L	0	X_L
Expectation	$(F + X_L)/2$	$(X_H - F)/2$	$(X_H + X_L)/2$

On the other hand, it does not affect the payoff of the debt holder in the high state but changes the payoff in the low state by R_L. Let E, D, and V be the expected equity, debt, and firm values with additional investment. Then, each value becomes

$$E = (X_H - F + R_H)/2 - I,$$
$$D = (F + X_L + R_L)/2,$$
$$V = (X_H + X_L)/2 + (R_H + R_L)/2 - I.$$

Table 4.2 presents each stakeholder's value with and without additional investment. If $R_H/2 - I > 0$, $E > E_0$. Then, the owner invests in this project, although the project reduces firm value. This outcome is called *risk shifting* (Jensen & Meckling, 1976). This result means that the owner can invest in an unprofitable project when the project yields a relatively high return in the high state. This is because the owner can shift the downside risk of the project to the debt holder as his value is neutral to his investment in the low state in which the firm defaults.

If there is no debt, $E = V = (X_H + X_L)/2 + (R_H + R_L)/2 - I < (X_H + X_L)/2 = V_0 = E_0$. The owner never invests in this project.

These two results suggest that debt can distort the incentives of a firm's decision maker if default is possible. It could induce underinvestment (debt overhang) or overinvestment (risk shifting), depending on the context. The next model explores when debt overhang is likely to occur and when risk shifting is likely to happen.

4.4 Debt overhang and risk shifting

Spiegel (2016) introduced a model that allowed to analyze debt overhang and risk shifting jointly in a more realistic setting, based on Berkovitch and Kim (1990). There are three periods in the model. In the beginning, a manager starts the firm by issuing debt with face value F. In the middle, cash flow X is realized. Then, the firm's equity holder determines the amount of investment I. In the end, investment yields $zg(I)$ and F is due, where $g(I)$ is strictly increasing, concave, $g(0) = 0$, $\lim_{I \to 0} g'(I) = \infty$, and $\lim_{I \to \infty} g'(I) = 0$. z is nonnegative and stochastic, following H, where H is the CDF of z. For the rest of the model, I consider two cases: (1) when the firm has enough cash in the middle (X exceeds investment amount) and (2) when the firm has a deficiency in cash in the middle (X is lower than investment amount).

Suppose the firm has excess cash in the middle so that the equity holder does not have to fund investment. The firm is solvent in the end if and only if $zg(I) + X - I \geq F \Leftrightarrow z \geq z_1$, where $z_1 = (F + I - X)/g(I)$. As the equity holder receives 0 when the firm is insolvent and a residual value when the firm is solvent, the expected value of equity is

$$E_1(F) = \int_{z_1}^{\infty} (zg(I) + X - I - F)dH(z).$$

Note the marginal net value of investment $\partial E_1(F)/\partial I$ is ∞ at $I = 0$. As the marginal increase in investment raises the value of equity at $I = 0$, there is no corner equilibrium. Thus, if there is an equilibrium, the equilibrium has to be interior—the first-order condition is a necessary condition for equilibrium. Then, the equilibrium level of investment I_1 satisfies the first-order condition. In particular, using the Leibniz rule,[3] it is expressed by

$$\frac{\partial E_1(F)}{\partial I} = \int_{z_1}^{\infty} (zg'(I_1) - 1)dH(z),$$

$$= g'(I_1) \int_{z_1}^{\infty} zdH(z) - (1 - H(z_1)),$$

$$= 0.$$

Then, it is equivalent to

$$g'(I_1) = E[z|z \geq z_1]^{-1}. \tag{4.7}$$

The debt holder receives all the firm's value when the firm is insolvent and face value when the firm is solvent. The expected value of the firm, that is, the sum of the expected equity and debt holders' values, is

$$V_1(F) = \underbrace{\int_{z_1}^{\infty} (zg(I) + X - I - F)dH(z)}_{\text{equity}} + \underbrace{\int_{0}^{z_1} (zg(I) + X - I)dH(z) + \int_{z_1}^{\infty} FdH(z)}_{\text{debt}},$$

$$= \int_{0}^{\infty} (zg(I) + X - I)dH(z),$$

$$= E[z]g(I) + X - I.$$

Next, suppose the firm has deficiency in cash in the middle so that the equity holder funds investment. The firm is solvent in the end if and only if $zg(I) \geq F \Leftrightarrow z \geq z_2$, where $z_2 = F/g(I)$. The equity holder receives 0 when the firm is insolvent and residual value when the firm is solvent. Also, the equity holder pays extra finance required for investment before the firm's solvency/insolvency state realizes. The expected equity holder's value is therefore

$$E_2(F) = \int_{z_2}^{\infty} (zg(I) - F)dH(z) - \underbrace{(I - X)}_{\text{extra finance to cover deficit}}.$$

Note that the marginal net value of investment $\partial E_2(F)/\partial I$ is ∞ at $I = 0$. As in the previous case, the first-order condition is necessary condition for an equilibrium. Then, the equilibrium level of investment, I_2, satisfies the following first-order condition:

$$\frac{\partial E_2(F)}{\partial I} = \int_{z_2}^{\infty} zg'(I_2)dH(z) - 1,$$

$$= g'(I_2) \int_{z_2}^{\infty} zdH(z) - 1,$$

$$= 0.$$

It is equivalent to

$$g'(I_2) = \int_{z_2}^{\infty} zdH(z)^{-1}. \tag{4.8}$$

The expected value of the firm is

$$V_2(F) = \underbrace{\int_{z_2}^{\infty} (zg(I) - F)dH(z) - (I - X)}_{\text{equity}} + \underbrace{\int_{0}^{z_2} zg(I)dH(z) + \int_{z_2}^{\infty} FdH(z)}_{\text{debt}},$$

$$= \int_{0}^{\infty} (zg(I) + X - I)dH(z),$$

$$= E[z]g(I) + X - I.$$

As suggested by this result, the firm's value is the same, regardless of the two cases. How much is the efficient level of investment for society? Let the firm's value be $V(F)$, where $V(F) = V_1(F) = V_2(F)$. Note the marginal net social value of investment $\partial V(F)/\partial I$ is ∞ at $I = 0$ and -1 at $I = \infty$. Also, $\partial V(F)/\partial I$ is strictly decreasing in I. Then, there is the unique efficient level of investment I_0 satisfying the first-order condition:

$$\frac{\partial V(F)}{\partial I} = E[z]g'(I_0) - 1,$$

$$= 0.$$

It is equivalent to

$$g'(I_0) = E[z]^{-1}. \tag{4.9}$$

Now, let us compare the equilibrium level of investment in the presence of excess cash I_1, the corresponding level in the presence of cash deficiency I_2, and the socially optimal level I_0. Each condition is characterized by the solution of equations (4.7), (4.8), and (4.9), respectively. For each problem, the left-hand side is the same and strictly decreasing in I. For any I, $\int_{z_2}^{\infty} z dH(z) \leq \int_0^{\infty} z dH(z) = E[z]$ and $\int_0^{\infty} z dH(z) = E[z] \leq E[z|z \geq z_1]$. Then, for any I, the right-hand side of each equation is ranked as $\int_{z_2}^{\infty} z dH(z)^{-1} \geq E[z]^{-1}$ and $E[z]^{-1} \geq E[z|z \geq z_1]^{-1}$.

Through proof by contradiction, comparing each level of investment is possible. Suppose $I_1 < I_0$. $g'(I_1) > g'(I_0)$. Then, equations (4.7) and (4.9) suggest that $E[z|z \geq z_1]^{-1} > E[z]^{-1}$, which contradicts one of the earlier inequalities. Similarly, suppose $I_2 > I_0$. $g'(I_2) < g'(I_0)$. Then, equations (4.8) and (4.9) suggest that $\int_{z_2}^{\infty} z dH(z)^{-1} < E[z]^{-1}$, which contradicts the other inequality. Based on these observations, the following claim holds:

- **Debt overhang and risk shifting by cash availability:** $I_2 \leq I_0 \leq I_1$.

Figure 4.5 presents equations (4.7) through (4.9) and the relative size of I_0, I_1, and I_2. This result suggests that excess cash can induce overinvestment. This is because the equity holder does not have to invest his or her own money in the project as it is mainly funded by the debt holder. The equity holder does not lose much in the bad state but earns a lot in the good state if he or she gambles. It also suggests that cash deficiency can induce underinvestment. In this case, the equity holder needs to invest his or her

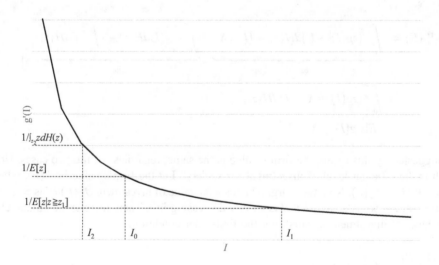

Figure 4.5 Equilibrium Level of Investment

own money in the project. Realizing that with some probability the project will not yield enough, he or she has an incentive to reduce investment.

4.5 Discussion

The agency theory backs up the weakness of the trade-off theory. It justifies the use of debt even in the absence of a corporate tax. Indeed, debt finance mitigates agency problem by aligning the incentives of a firm's decision maker and a firm value maximizer. If default is possible, debt finance can still distort the incentives of a firm's decision maker through debt overhang and risk shifting. In this respect, the agency theory not only proposes the competing hypothesis against the tax benefit of debt but also suggests a deeper level of inefficiency caused by default beyond the cost of default proposed by the trade-off theory.

By nature, the agency theory involves strategic interactions of multiple firm stakeholders. This approach naturally provokes the idea of associating capital structure choice with game theory, contracting, and mechanism design. The progress of microeconomic theory during the late 1970s and 1980s allows researchers to analyze corporate capital structure from the perspective of a principal–agent model, a contract theory, and a mechanism design. The next chapter covers capital structure theories proposed by microeconomic theorists.

Notes

1 Here, I show a simplified version introduced by Spiegel (2016).
2 R_L can be negative.
3 In general, the rule suggests that

$$\frac{d}{dx}\left(\int_{a(x)}^{b(x)} f(x,t)dt\right) = f(x,b(x))\frac{db(x)}{dx} - f(x,a(x))\frac{da(x)}{dx} + \int_{a(x)}^{b(x)} \frac{\partial f(x,t)}{\partial x}dt.$$

Bibliography

Berkovitch, E. and Kim, E. H. (1990). Financial contracting and leverage induced over- and under-investment incentives. *Journal of Finance*, 45(3):765–94.

Jensen, M. C. and Meckling, W. H. (1976). Theory of the firm: Managerial behavior, agency costs and ownership structure. *Journal of Financial Economics*, 3(4):305–60.

Myers, S. C. (1977). Determinants of corporate borrowing. *Journal of Financial Economics*, 5 (2):147–75.

Spiegel, Y. (2016). *TAU Corporate Finance–Semester alef 2016–17, Topic 3: Agency models of capital structure*.

5

SECURITY DESIGN

5.1 Overview

In this chapter, I show an alternative approach of explaining the wide use of debt, utilizing the rapid progress of the contract theory in microeconomics. In particular, I claim that debt can be an optimal financial contract in the presence of various contractual frictions.

5.2 Optimal risk-sharing with moral hazard

Hölmstrom (1979) and Harris and Raviv (1979) published the similar model in the same year to analyze principal–agent (PA) contracts. In the model, the investor makes a take-it-or-leave-it offer to a manager with outside reservation $\underline{U}$. If the offered contract is accepted, the manager chooses an action $a \in \mathbb{R}^{++}$,[1] which will have an effect on cash flow $x \in X$, where $X = [\underline{x}, \bar{x}]$ and $\underline{x} < \bar{x}$. I denote the interior of X by X°. Because cash flow is verifiable, the investor writes a contract contingent on x. The manager receives $w(x)$ as a wage, where $w(x) \in \mathbb{R}$. The monetary utility of the investor is $V(x - w(x))$, where $V' > 0 \geq V''$. The manager's utility is $U(w(x), a) = u(w(x)) - a$, where $u' > 0 \geq u''$. The investor is risk-neutral if $V(.)$ is an identity function, whereas the manager is risk-neutral if $u(.)$ is an identity function.

The model assumes the distribution of cash flow is dependent on managerial efforts specified by action a. Let the cumulative distribution function (CDF) of X be $F(x, a)$ and the probability density function (PDF) of X be $f(x, a)$. Then, it satisfies $F_a(x, a) < 0$ for $\forall x \in X^{\circ}$, where F_a (f_a) is partial derivative of F (f) with respect to a, meaning an increase in a leads to the first-order stochastic dominance (FOSD) increase of X. Also, $F(\underline{x}, a) = 0, F(\bar{x}, a) = 1$ for any a.[2] Due to this assumption, the support of a cash flow does not depend on a. I call this assumption fixed support (FS).

One example of CDF satisfying FOSD and FS is $F(x, a) = x^a$, where $X = [0, 1]$. Then, $F_a(x, a) = x^a \ln(x) < 0$ for $\forall x \in (0, 1)$. Also, $F(x, a) = x^a|_{x=0} = 0$ and $F(x, a) = x^a|_{x=1} = 1$ for any a. Figure 5.1 presents the two distributions of this form, where $a > a'$. Indeed, the figure shows the two distributions have the common support and $F(x, a) < F(x, a')$ for $\forall x \in (0, 1)$.

The first-order stochastic dominance property of a cash flow with respect to managerial efforts means that an increase in managerial effort level raises the cash flow on average. In general, I can prove the following:

- **FOSD:** Assume FOSD and FS. $E[g(x)|a] > E[g(x)|a']$, if $a > a'$ and $g(x)$ is a strictly increasing function.

28

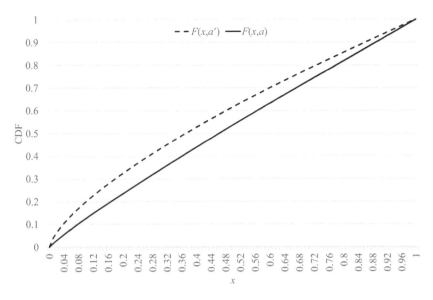

Figure 5.1 Distributions Satisfying FOSD and FS

To see why, let $y(x) = F^{-1}(F(x, a'), a)$. Then, (1) $y(x) > x, \forall x \in (\underline{x}, \bar{x})$; (2) $y(\underline{x}) = \underline{x}$, $y(\bar{x}) = \bar{x}$; (3) $y(x)$ strictly increases in x. Among these three properties, (2) and (3) seem almost obvious. Property (1) is also immediate by showing the definition of $y(x)$ graphically. Figure 5.2 presents how $y(x)$ is defined. Indeed, (1) holds. Therefore,

$$\int_{\underline{x}}^{\bar{x}} g(x)dF(x, a)$$

$$= \int_{\underline{x}}^{\bar{x}} g(y(x))dF(y(x), a) \quad \text{from integration by substitution with (2) and (3)}$$

$$= \int_{\underline{x}}^{\bar{x}} g(y(x))dF(x, a') \quad \text{from definition}$$

$$> \int_{\underline{x}}^{\bar{x}} g(x)dF(x, a') \quad \text{from (1) and (2).}$$

This completes the proof of the claim.

I start with the case in which managerial efforts are observable, meaning that the investor is able to enforce the manager to induce the predetermined effort level.[3] Given that the manager has the outside option, the investor's problem is to maximize his surplus subject to the manager's participation constraint. Such a participation constraint is often called the individual rationality (IR) constraint. Then, the investor's optimization problem is

$$\max{}_{w(.),a} \int_{\underline{x}}^{\bar{x}} V(x - w(x))f(x, a)dx$$

$$\text{s.t. } \int_{\underline{x}}^{\bar{x}} u(w(x))f(x, a)dx - a \geq \underline{U}. \quad \text{[IR]}$$

Here, the investor tries to maximize the expected surplus by choosing the optimal wage for each x and the managerial effort level. Using the Lagrangian where

$$L(w(.), a, \lambda) = \int_{\underline{x}}^{\bar{x}} [V(x - w(x)) + \lambda u(w(x))]f(x, a)dx - \lambda a - \lambda \underline{U},$$

29

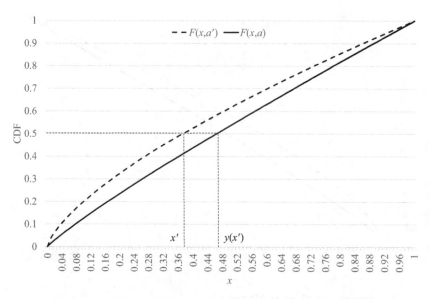

Figure 5.2 Graphical Presentation of (1)

Note: $F(x', a') = F(y(x'), a) = 0.5$.

the first-order condition is obtained by

$$\forall x \in X, \frac{V'(x - w(x))}{u'(w(x))} = \lambda, \tag{5.1}$$

$$\int_{\underline{x}}^{\bar{x}} [V(x - w(x)) + \lambda u(w(x))] f_a(x, a) dx = \lambda, \tag{5.2}$$

IR binds.

Notice that this condition is necessary. The optimal contract and effort level are interior as they are chosen from an open set. Also, notice that IR binds at the optimal contract—otherwise, slightly reducing the manager's payoff would raise the investor's expected surplus.

From the preceding, I can draw a couple of facts. If $V' = 1$, $u'' < 0$, $w(x)$ has to be a constant. If $u' = 1$, $V'' < 0$, $x - w(x)$ has to be a constant.

Moreover, suppose both are risk-averse ($u'' < 0$, $V'' < 0$). If $w(x)$ weakly decreases in x, the left-hand side of equation (5.1) strictly decreases in x and never becomes constant. Therefore, $w(x)$ has to strictly increase in x. If $x - w(x)$ weakly decreases in x, the left-hand side of equation (5.1) strictly increases in x, as $w(x)$ strictly increases in x, and never becomes constant. Thus, $x - w(x)$ has to strictly increase in x as well.

Combining these findings, I characterize the optimal financial contract under observable managerial efforts (first-best contract) as follows.

- **Optimal risk-sharing (first-best):** If the investor is risk-neutral and the manager is risk-averse ($V' = 1$, $u'' < 0$), $w(x)$ is induced to be a constant. If both the investor and the manager are risk-averse ($u'' < 0$, $V'' < 0$), both $w(x)$ and $x - w(x)$ are induced to strictly increase in x. If the manager is risk-neutral and the investor is risk-averse ($u' = 1$, $V'' < 0$), the induced contract has the form of $w(x) = x + k$, where k is some constant.

I summarize the implication from this result for the rest of the paragraph. If the investor is risk-neutral and the manager is risk-averse, the investor's surplus increases when the investor takes a risk. By making the manager's wealth risk-free, the investor is able to save the risk premium required for the manager to agree with the contract. Then, equity finance, from which the investor receives a residual claim, is optimal. On the other hand, if the investor is risk-averse and the manager is risk-neutral, the investor's surplus increases when the manager takes a risk. By making the investor's wealth risk-free, the investor is able to save utility loss from taking risk. Then, debt finance, from which the investor receives a fixed claim, is optimal. When both are risk-averse, both share the risk of the cash flow. Then, the optimal contract is somewhere between debt and equity. The payoff of the investor is still positively associated with the cash flow, so it is distinct from debt. However, it is not as perfect as equity, because an increase in cash flow does not raise the payoff of the investor as much as it raises the payoff of an equity holder.

Rewriting the first-order condition,[4]

$$1$$
$$= \int_{\underline{x}}^{\bar{x}} [(V(x - w(x))/\lambda) + u(w(x))] f_a(x, a) dx$$
$$= \underbrace{([(V(x - w(x))/\lambda) + u(w(x))] F_a(x, a))|_{\underline{x}}^{\bar{x}}}_{\text{0 by } F_a(\underline{x},a)=F_a(\bar{x},a)=0}$$
$$- \int_{\underline{x}}^{\bar{x}} \left[\begin{array}{c} \underbrace{(V'(x - w(x))/\lambda)}_{u'(w(x)) \text{ by equation (5.1)}} (1 - w'(x)) \\ + u'(w(x)) w'(x) \end{array} \right] F_a(x, a) dx \quad \text{from integration by parts}$$
$$= \quad\quad - \int_{\underline{x}}^{\bar{x}} u'(w(x)) F_a(x, a) dx.$$

In particular, the optimal level of managerial efforts becomes simpler if the manager is risk-neutral. Indeed,

$$1$$
$$= -\int_{\underline{x}}^{\bar{x}} u'(w(x)) F_a(x, a) dx \quad\quad \text{from the above}$$
$$= \quad -\int_{\underline{x}}^{\bar{x}} F_a(x, a) dx \quad\quad \text{from the proposition}$$
$$= -(x F_a(x, a))|_{\underline{x}}^{\bar{x}} + \int_{\underline{x}}^{\bar{x}} x f_a(x, a) dx \quad \text{from integration by parts}$$
$$= \quad \partial E[x|a]/\partial a.$$

This equation suggests that induced managerial efforts are set to the level at which the marginal cost of increasing effort level is equal to the marginal value of increasing effort level for a society (marginal increase in an expected cash flow).

31

Therefore, I claim the following:

- **Efficiency:** Assume FS. If the manager is risk-neutral, induced a is efficient.

This completes the analysis of the first-best contract under which the investor observes managerial efforts.

When managerial efforts are unobservable for the investor, he cannot enforce the manager to choose the first-best level he solved in the earlier problem. In this case, he needs to consider the second-best choice in which the effort level is set to be optimal for the manager given contract $w(.)$, which is called an incentive-compatibility constraint. Then, his problem is to maximize his surplus subject to the manager's incentive compatibility (IC) constraint as well as the participation constraint (IR). Then, the investor's optimization problem is

$$\max_{w(.),a} \int_{\underline{x}}^{\bar{x}} V(x - w(x))f(x,a)dx$$

s.t. $\int_{\underline{x}}^{\bar{x}} u(w(x))f(x,a)dx - a \geq \underline{U}$ [IR]

$a \in \arg\max_{a' \in \mathbb{R}^{++}} \int_{\underline{x}}^{\bar{x}} u(w(x))f(x,a')dx - a'.$ [IC]

This problem, however, is hard to solve, as the IC constraint is intricate. One solution is to relax IC constraint: the effort level has to only satisfy the first-order condition of the manager's objective function. This method is called the first-order approach (FOA). In general, the first-order condition is only necessary, not sufficient—it just enforces the effort level at which the manager's expected utility is at a stationary point. To resolve this issue, Rogerson (1985) specifies the conditions under which the solution of the FOA is same as that of the previous problem:

- **FOA:** If the distribution of a cash flow satisfies the monotone likelihood ratio property (MLRP) and the convexity of cumulative distribution function (CDFC) as well as the FOSD and FS:

$$d(f_a(x,a)/f(x,a))/dx > 0, \forall x \in X^\circ, \quad \text{[MLRP]}$$
$$F_{aa}(x,a) \geq 0, \forall x \in X^\circ, \quad\quad \text{[CDFC]}$$

where $F_{aa}(f_{aa})$ is the second derivative with respect to a, the FOA is valid when $u'' < 0$.[5]

I prove this claim using the discussion in a later part of this section. For this purpose, suppose FOSD, FS, MLRP, CDFC, and $u'' < 0$.

I start by considering the second-best contract under the "doubly relaxed" constraint:[6]

$$\int_{\underline{x}}^{\bar{x}} u(w(x))f_a(x,a)dx - 1 \geq 0.$$

Then, the Lagrangian becomes equivalent to equation (5.3) in the later part of this section. Its first-order condition is hence equivalent to equations (5.6) and (5.7). The multiplier for the doubly relaxed constraint μ is nonnegative.

If the multiplier is positive, equation (5.4) is satisfied. The MLRP suggests that the induced wage contract increases the cash flow as discussed in a later part of this section. Then, I can show that inequality (5.5) holds under the CDFC, implying the optimality of the manager. Indeed, using integration by parts,

$$\int_{\underline{x}}^{\bar{x}} u(w(x))f_{aa}(x,a)dx = \underbrace{u(w(x))F_{aa}(x,a)\big|_{\underline{x}}^{\bar{x}}}_{0 \text{ from FS}} - \int_{\underline{x}}^{\bar{x}} u'(w(x))w'(x)F_{aa}(x,a)dx$$

$$= -\int_{\underline{x}}^{\bar{x}} \underbrace{u'(w(x))w'(x)}_{\text{nonnegative}} \quad \underbrace{F_{aa}(x,a)}_{\text{nonnegative from CDFC}} \quad dx$$

$$\leq 0.$$

In this way, the second-order condition for the optimality of the manager is satisfied.

If μ is zero, the first-best contract becomes the induced wage contract. Then, from the outcome about the first-best contract, $0 \leq w'(x) < 1$ as $u'' < 0$. Because $V(x - w(x))$ strictly increases in x,

$$\int_{\underline{x}}^{\bar{x}} V(x - w(x))f_a(x,a)dx > 0,$$

under FOSD. Also, notice that

$$\lambda\left(\int_{\underline{x}}^{\bar{x}} u(w(x))f_a(x,a)dx - 1\right) \geq 0,$$

where λ is the multiplier associated with IR. Then, the left-hand side of equation (5.7) is positive, which violates equation (5.7). Thus, μ is positive.

Because equation (5.4) is satisfied, the solution subject to the doubly relaxed constraint matches the solution under the FOA. Then, because the solution subject to the doubly relaxed constraint satisfies inequality (5.5), the solution under the FOA also satisfies inequality (5.5). Thus, this result suggests the solution to the investor's optimization problem subject to the first-order condition of the manager's optimality (the FOA) matches that subject to both the first-order and second-order conditions of the manager's optimality. The solution under the FOA maximizes the investor's surplus subject to the *necessary* and *sufficient* condition of the manager's optimality, which completes the proof.

Assuming FOSD, FS, MLRP, CDFC, and $u'' < 0$, I use the FOA to solve this problem. Then, the Lagrangian becomes

$$L(w(.), a, \lambda, \mu^+, \mu^-) = \int_{\underline{x}}^{\bar{x}} [V(x - w(x)) + \lambda u(w(x))]f(x,a)dx - \lambda a - \lambda\underline{U}$$

$$+\mu^+\left[\int_{\underline{x}}^{\bar{x}} u(w(x))f_a(x,a)dx - 1\right]$$

$$+\mu^-\left[1 - \int_{\underline{x}}^{\bar{x}} u(w(x))f_a(x,a)dx\right].$$

The last two terms correspond to the constraints:

$$\int_{\underline{x}}^{\bar{x}} u(w(x))f_a(x,a)dx - 1 \geq 0,$$

$$\int_{\underline{x}}^{\bar{x}} u(w(x))f_a(x,a)dx - 1 \leq 0.$$

Satisfying both conditions is equivalent to satisfying the FOC of the manager. This Lagrangian is simplified to

$$L(w(.),a,\lambda,\mu) = \int_{\underline{x}}^{\bar{x}} [V(x - w(x)) + \lambda u(w(x))]f(x,a)dx - \lambda a - \lambda \underline{U}$$

$$+\mu \left[\int_{\underline{x}}^{\bar{x}} u(w(x))f_a(x,a)dx - 1\right],$$

(5.3)

where $\mu = \mu^+ - \mu^-$. Because μ^+ and μ^- are both nonnegative, the sign of μ is ambiguous.

IR binds at the optimal contract as in the previous problem. IC binds by setting, and, if the FOA is valid, the second-order condition of the manager is satisfied, implying

$$\int_{\underline{x}}^{\bar{x}} u(w(x))f_a(x,a)dx - 1 = 0,$$

(5.4)

$$\int_{\underline{x}}^{\bar{x}} u(w(x))f_{aa}(x,a)dx \leq 0.$$

(5.5)

The first-order condition for the investor is

$$\forall x \in X, \frac{V'(x - w(x))}{u'(x - (x - w(x)))} = \lambda + \mu \frac{f_a(x,a)}{f(x,a)},$$

(5.6)

$$\int_{\underline{x}}^{\bar{x}} V(x - w(x))f_a(x,a)dx$$

$$+\lambda \underbrace{\left[\int_{\underline{x}}^{\bar{x}} u(w(x))f_a(x,a)dx - 1\right]}_{\text{0 from equation (5.4)}}$$

(5.7)

$$+\mu \underbrace{\left[\int_{\underline{x}}^{\bar{x}} u(w(x))f_{aa}(x,a)dx\right]}_{\leq 0 \text{ from inequality (5.5)}} = 0,$$

IR binds.

For convenience, I define $w_\lambda(x)$ as

$$\frac{V'(x - w_\lambda(x))}{u'(x - (x - w_\lambda(x)))} = \lambda.$$

(5.8)

Suppose $x - w_\lambda(x)$ weakly decreases in x. As the manager is risk-averse ($u'' < 0$), an increase in x weakly raises the numerator and strictly reduces the denominator in the left-hand side of equation (5.8), strictly raising the left-hand side of equation (5.8). This result is not consistent with the fact that the right-hand side is constant. Thus, $x - w_\lambda(x)$ strictly increases in x.

Now, I would like to determine the sign of the Lagrange multiplier μ. To determine this sign, suppose $\mu \leq 0$. Then, if $f_a(x, a) \geq 0$,

$$
\begin{aligned}
\frac{V'(x - w(x))}{u'(x - (x - w(x)))} &= \lambda + \mu \frac{f_a(x, a)}{f(x, a)} \\
&\leq \frac{V'(x - w_\lambda(x))}{u'(x - (x - w_\lambda(x)))}.
\end{aligned}
$$

Therefore, $x - w(x) \geq x - w_\lambda(x)$. If $f_a(x, a) \leq 0$,

$$
\begin{aligned}
\frac{V'(x - w(x))}{u'(x - (x - w(x)))} &= \lambda + \mu \frac{f_a(x, a)}{f(x, a)} \\
&\geq \frac{V'(x - w_\lambda(x))}{u'(x - (x - w_\lambda(x)))}.
\end{aligned}
$$

Therefore, $x - w(x) \leq x - w_\lambda(x)$. From these two facts,

$$
\int_{\underline{x}}^{\bar{x}} V(x - w(x)) f_a(x, a) dx \geq \int_{\underline{x}}^{\bar{x}} V(x - w_\lambda(x)) f_a(x, a) dx.
$$

Considering FOSD and $V(x - w_\lambda(x))$ strictly increases in x as $x - w_\lambda(x)$ strictly increases in x,

$$
\int_{\underline{x}}^{\bar{x}} V(x - w_\lambda(x)) f_a(x, a) dx = \frac{\partial E[V(x - w_\lambda(x))|a]}{\partial a}
$$

$$
> 0.
$$

Then, I conclude

$$
\int_{\underline{x}}^{\bar{x}} V(x - w(x)) f_a(x, a) dx > 0.
$$

The second term of the left-hand side of equation (5.7) is 0. The third term is nonnegative as $\mu \leq 0$. Then, the left-hand side of equation (5.7) is strictly positive as the first term is strictly positive from the earlier inequality. Thus, equation (5.7) does not hold. This proves $\mu > 0$.

Now, let us analyze equation (5.6). Due to the MLRP and $\mu > 0$, the right-hand side of equation (5.6) strictly increases in x. The left-hand side of equation (5.6) hence strictly increases in x. If $w(x)$ weakly decreased in x, the left-hand side of equation (5.6) would weakly decrease in x as well, which is a contradiction. Thus, $w(x)$ strictly increases in x.

If the manager is risk-neutral ($u' = 1$, $u'' = 0$), the first-best effort level satisfies IC. To see why, let us characterize IC under the first-best contract:

$$a \in \arg\max_{a' \in \mathbb{R}^{++}} \int_{\underline{x}}^{\bar{x}} u(w(x))f(x, a')dx - a'$$

$$= \arg\max_{a' \in \mathbb{R}^{++}} \int_{\underline{x}}^{\bar{x}} (x + k)f(x, a')dx - a'$$

$$= \arg\max_{a' \in \mathbb{R}^{++}} \int_{\underline{x}}^{\bar{x}} xf(x, a')dx - a'$$

$$= \arg\max_{a' \in \mathbb{R}^{++}} E[x|a'] - a'.$$

The previous proposition suggests that the first-best effort level maximizes $E[x|a'] - a'$, so it satisfies the preceding condition. Thus, the first-best contract becomes second-best as well.

Finally, I prove that the MLRP is sufficient for FOSD under FS. Because $d(f_a(x, a)/f(x, a))/dx > 0$ for $\forall x \in X^\circ$, $f_a(x, a)/f(x, a)$ is positive if x is greater than some threshold $x' \in X^\circ$, where $f_a(x', a)/f(x', a) = 0$, and $f_a(x, a)/f(x, a)$ is negative if x is smaller than x'. Alternatively, $f_a(x, a)/f(x, a) > 0$ for $\forall x > \underline{x}$ or $f_a(x, a)/f(x, a) < 0$ for $\forall x < \bar{x}$. Suppose $x \in X^\circ$, where $x \geq x'$ or $f_a(x, a)/f(x, a) > 0$ for $\forall x > \underline{x}$. Then,

$$F_a(x, a)$$
$$= \quad F_a(x, a) - F_a(\underline{x}, a)$$
$$= \quad \int_{\underline{x}}^{x} f_a(x, a)dx$$
$$= \int_{\underline{x}}^{x} (f_a(x, a)/f(x, a))f(x, a)dx$$
$$< \int_{\underline{x}}^{\bar{x}} (f_a(x, a)/f(x, a))f(x, a)dx$$
$$= \quad \int_{\underline{x}}^{\bar{x}} f_a(x, a)dx$$
$$= \quad F_a(\bar{x}, a) - F_a(\underline{x}, a)$$
$$= \quad 0.$$

Suppose $x \in X^\circ$, where $x < x'$ or $f_a(x, a)/f(x, a) < 0$ for $\forall x < \bar{x}$. Then,

$$F_a(x, a)$$
$$= \quad F(x, a) - F_a(\underline{x}, a)$$
$$= \quad \int_{\underline{x}}^{x} f_a(x, a)dx$$
$$= \int_{\underline{x}}^{x} (f_a(x, a)/f(x, a))f(x, a)dx$$
$$< \quad 0.$$

Therefore, $\forall x \in X^\circ$, $F_a(x, a) < 0$. Thus, the MLRP implies FOSD under FS.

I summarize our findings in the following proposition:

36

- **Optimal risk-sharing (second-best):** Assume FS, MLRP, and CDFC. If the manager is risk-averse ($u'' < 0$, $V'' \le 0$), $w(x)$ is induced to strictly increase in x. If the manager is risk-neutral and the investor is risk-averse ($u' = 1$, $V'' < 0$), the induced contract is same as the first-best contract.

Unlike the first-best contract, the second-best contract requires the manager to share risk even if the investor is risk-neutral. This is because performance-sensitive pay is needed to induce the manager to make efforts. As a result, the manager's wage strictly increases in x, even if she is risk-averse. Unlike in the first-best contract, the investor has to sacrifice some risk premium as the manager shares some risk, which reduces the surplus of the investor. On the other hand, the manager's pay should be perfectly aligned with the cash flow from the perspective of both risk-sharing and effort-inducing when the manager is risk-neutral. Consequently, the first-best contract, $w(x) = x + k$, is still the second-best one.

The remaining question is whether the distribution satisfying FS, MLRP, and CDFC really exists. In fact, the previous example of CDF ($F(x, a) = x^a$) satisfies the MLRP and CDFC as well. The MLRP holds because, for $\forall x \in X^\circ$,

$$d(f_a(x,a)/f(x,a))/dx$$
$$= d((x^{a-1} + \ln(x)ax^{a-1})/ax^{a-1})/dx$$
$$= d((1 + a\ln(x))/a)/dx$$
$$> 0.$$

Moreover, CDFC holds because, for $\forall x \in X^\circ$,

$$F_{aa}(x,a)$$
$$= (\ln(x))^2 x^a$$
$$\ge 0.$$

Thus, the previous example of the CDF satisfies the FS, MLRP, and CDFC. This result suggests that the investor's optimal contract has a constant payoff stream, *regardless of action observability*, as long as the manager is risk-neutral. Figure 5.3 presents the optimal investor's payoff schedule when the manager is risk-neutral. The optimal payoff of the investor depicted in the figure captures an important aspect of debt contract: the payoff of an investor tends to be insensitive to a firm's cash flow.

However, a debt's payoff structure is not flat on all the ranges of cash flows in reality. Typically, when a firm's cash flow falls below a certain threshold, a debt holder seizes the assets and his payoff becomes perfectly aligned with a firm's cash flow in practice. The optimal payoff schedule predicted by this preceding model cannot capture this feature.

In the next section, I briefly review the extension by Innes (1990). The model successfully rationalizes a concave payoff structure of debt by imposing additional frictions.

5.3 Financial contract under limited liability

Innes (1990) extends the previous model by considering the case in which a risk-neutral manager offers a take-it-or-leave-it offer to a risk-neutral investor. The manager needs a predetermined amount of I for investment ($I > 0$). We assume that this investment is feasible in

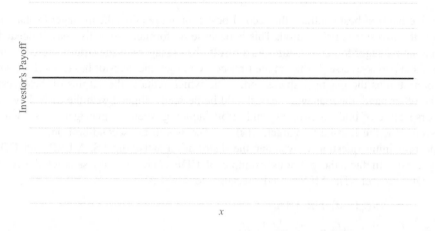

Figure 5.3 Optimal Risk-Sharing With the Risk-Neutral Manager

the sense that expected cash flow exceeds I for any level of effort specified by arbitrary action a. The risk-free rate is zero, so the investor is willing to invest if the net expected return is nonnegative. The investor receives payoff $r(x)$. The manager receives a residual claim and incurs the cost of making an effort, so he receives $x - r(x) - a$. I keep using the same notations and assumptions (FS, MLRP, and CDFC) for the distribution of a cash flow, where $\underline{x} \geq 0$.

The manager's optimization problem is

$$\max{}_{r(.),a} \int_{\underline{x}}^{\bar{x}} (x - r(x))f(x,a)dx - a$$

s.t. $$\int_{\underline{x}}^{\bar{x}} r(x)f(x,a)dx \geq I \qquad \text{[IR]}$$

$$a \in \arg\max{}_{a' \in \mathbb{R}^{++}} \int_{\underline{x}}^{\bar{x}} (x - r(x))f(x,a')dx - a'. \qquad \text{[IC]}$$

Note, as in the previous section, IC requires the effort level chosen by the manager to maximize the manager's expected surplus given contract $r(.)$. As in the proof of validity for FOA, I replace IC by the doubly relaxed constraint: $\int_{\underline{x}}^{\bar{x}} (x - r(x))f_a(x,a)dx - 1 \geq 0$. Under this constraint, the manager cannot offer a contract under which he has an incentive to shirk ex post. The Lagrangian under the doubly relaxed constraint is

$$L(r(.),a,\lambda,\mu) = \int_{\underline{x}}^{\bar{x}} [(x - r(x)) + \lambda r(x)]f(x,a)dx - a - \lambda I$$

$$+ \mu \left[\int_{\underline{x}}^{\bar{x}} (x - r(x))f_a(x,a)dx - 1 \right].$$

The partial derivative of the Lagrangean with respect to contract $r(.)$ satisfies

$$\forall x \in X, \frac{dL}{dr} \quad \propto \quad -1 + \lambda - \mu \frac{f_a(x,a)}{f(x,a)}. \tag{5.9}$$

Here, μ is nonnegative as it is the Lagrange multiplier. Assume $\mu > 0$. Because the MLRP suggests that $f_a(x, a)/f(x, a)$ strictly increases in x, equation (5.9) implies that there is no interior solution unless $x = x^*$, where $\lambda - 1 = \mu f_a(x^*, a)/f(x^*, a)$. If x is below x^*, $dL/dr > 0$. If x is above x^*, $dL/dr < 0$.

To resolve this issue, Innes (1990) introduces the limited liability constraint that assures each player receives a nonnegative payoff. Specifically, the optimal contract is subject to

$$r(x) \in [0, x]. \quad [LL]$$

Then, the optimal contract subject to LL has the corner solution:

$$r(x) = \begin{cases} x & \text{if } x \leq x^* \\ 0 & \text{if } x > x^* \end{cases}. \tag{5.10}$$

I first verify $\underline{x} < x^* < \bar{x}$. If $x^* \leq \underline{x}$, r does not satisfy IR. If $x^* \geq \bar{x}$, IR does not bind, so there is a chance of raising the surplus of the manager by reducing the payoff of the investor. Thus, $\underline{x} < x^* < \bar{x}$.

I next investigate when $\mu = 0$ is possible. Under LL and $\mu = 0$, $r(x) = 0$ or $r(x) = x$ or $\lambda = 1$. If $r(x) = 0$, IR is unsatisfied. If $r(x) = x$, IR does not bind so that there is a chance of raising the surplus of the manager by reducing the payoff of the investor. Then, $\lambda = 1$ and the manager would choose the socially optimal level of action. Thus, $\mu > 0$ if the efficient effort level is not induced.

When the efficient effort level is not induced, the doubly relaxed constraint binds at the optimal contract, because $\mu > 0$. In addition, FS, MLRP, and CDFC jointly suggest the second-order condition for the manager's optimality is satisfied. This claim is immediately clear if we replace $w(x)$ by $x - r(x)$ and $u(.)$ by an identity function in the proof of validity for FOA, given that $x - r(x)$ increases in x. Thus, the solution to the problem subject to the doubly relaxed constraint matches the solution to the manager's optimization problem in our interest, when the efficient effort level is not induced.

Consequently, this model suggests that the optimal financial contract is almost like debt, at least when the efficient effort level is not induced under the doubly relaxed constraint. Up to a certain threshold cash flow, the investor fully receives the cash flow. If a cash flow exceeds the threshold, the investor receives a flat payment. This feature is what the previous model misses. Figure 5.4 presents the payoff schedule of this contract. In turn, the manager receives a "live-or-die" wage contract.

The remaining issue is that the contract is still not monotonic though the payoff of debt is. To fill in the gap, the author introduces the so-called monotonicity constraint under which $r(x)$ weakly increases in x.

$$\forall x > x', \quad r(x) \geq r(x'). \quad [MN]$$

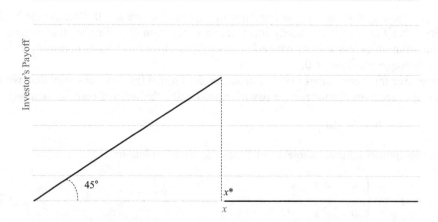

Figure 5.4 Optimal Contract Under Limited Liability

Note that a live-or-die wage contract is hard to implement in reality. For example, if the manager can revise profit reports upward around the threshold x^* through tiny (hence costless) borrowing, his wage can jump up from this manipulation. When this constraint binds, however, such a jump disappears from his wage schedule. Also, this constraint prevents the investor from blocking managerial profit-enhancing activities.

To satisfy this constraint while minimizing changes from the previous optimal contract, the new optimal contract has the payoff schedule of debt. In accordance with this intuition, Innes (1990) proves the optimal contract subject to LL and MN has the following structure:

$$ r(x) = \begin{cases} x & \text{if } x \le D \\ D & \text{if } x > D \end{cases}. \tag{5.11} $$

5.4 Financial contract under costly state verification

Townsend (1979) and Gale and Hellwig (1985) rationalize debt as the optimal financial contract in the presence of costly state verification (CSV). In one version of their model, as in Innes (1990), a risk-neutral manager offers a take-it-or-leave-it offer to a risk-neutral investor.[7] The manager needs a predetermined amount of I for investment ($I > 0$). The risk-free rate is zero, so the investor is willing to invest if the net expected return is nonnegative.

However, unlike Innes (1990), the investor cannot verify the firm's cash flow without paying cost. The investor can verify it only by paying fees K ($K > 0$). The manager reports y when the cash flow is x, where the support of the cash flow distribution is the set of nonnegative real numbers. Conditional on y, the investor determines the presence or absence of auditing $A(y)$ (= 1 if auditing, = 0 otherwise). Then, the investor receives $r(y)$

in the case of no auditing and $r_A(y, x)$ in the case of auditing. In turn, the manager receives $x - r(y)$ in the case of no auditing and $x - r_A(y, x)$ in the case of auditing. Because the outcome is contingent on the manager's report, this contract is considered as the mechanism.

According to the Revelation Principle (Myerson, 1979), I can restrict attention to contracts that provide an incentive for the manager to report a cash flow truthfully. Why? Suppose $r(y) = h(y)$ is the contract and $y = g(x)$ is the manager's report function induced by the contract. Then, consider the new contract $h^* = h \circ g$. As the manager can replicate the original outcome by setting his report equal to the cash flow under the new contract, $y = x$ is the manager's report function induced by the new contract. Thus, for each contract, there is a corresponding contract that yields the same outcome and incentivizes the manager to report a cash flow truthfully. In other words, when solving the optimal contract, it suffices to focus on the subset of contracts in which the manager reports cash flow truthfully.

Focusing on the set of financial contracts in which the manager reports a cash flow truthfully, the manager's optimization problem is

$$\max\nolimits_{A(.),r(.),r_A(.,.)} \int_0^\infty [(1 - A(x))(x - r(x)) + A(x)(x - r_A(x,x))]f(x)dx$$

s.t.
$$\int_0^\infty [(1 - A(x))r(x) + A(x)(r_A(x,x) - K)]f(x)dx \geq I \qquad \text{[IR]}$$

$$\forall x, r(x) \in [0,x], r_A(x,x) \in [0,x] \qquad \text{[LL]}$$

$$\forall x, x \in \arg \max\nolimits_y (1 - A(y))(x - r(y)) + A(y)(x - r_A(y,x)). \qquad \text{[IC]}$$

Under IC, truthful reporting becomes optimal for the manager. Being subject to IC, the investor limits the set of contracts to those in which the manager reports a cash flow truthfully. Because I limit attention to the contract where the manager reports cash flow truthfully, IR and the objective function are based on the report function $y = x$.

I then claim the following.

- **Optimal contract under CSV:** The solution to the preceding problem is the standard debt in which

$$A(x) = \begin{cases} 1 & \text{if } x \leq D \\ 0 & \text{if } x > D \end{cases},$$

$$r(x) = D,$$

$$r_A(x,x) = x.$$

I provide a sketch of proof in the following list. The proof comprises five steps:

1   The payoff to the investor has to be insensitive to cash flow in the absence of auditing. Otherwise, the manager would falsely report cash flow in order to raise his payoff, which violates IC. Consequently, $r(x) = D$.

2   The payoff to the investor in the audit region (the set of x where $A(x) = 1$) cannot exceed D. Otherwise, the manager would falsely report cash flow in the no-audit region (the set of x where $A(x) = 0$). Then, to satisfy IR, $D > 0$.

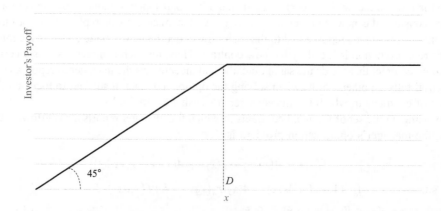

Figure 5.5 Optimal Contract Under Costly State Verification

3   To maximize the manager's surplus subject to IR, minimizing the audit cost and reducing the payoff to the investor is optimal. Note that having no audit region is inadmissible, because it violates LL when x is small. Then, paying full amount to the investor in the audit region reduces the audit region. Consequently, $r_A(x, x) = x$.

4   Given that the full payment to the investor is optimal in the audit region, $r_A(x, x) = x \leq D$ because of 2. Therefore, for any x in the audit region, $x \leq D$ holds.

5   If $\exists x' < D$ in the no-audit region, the contract violates LL. Therefore, such x' does not exist. This implies the audit region is the interval $[0, D]$.

Figure 5.5 presents the payoff schedule of this contract. As suggested by the figure, this result enables us to rationalize the prevalent use of debt when state verification is costly. In particular, the result is quite robust to the distrbution of cash flow, whereas the models based on the PA approach often require technical conditions on the distribution of cash flow.

5.5 Optimal allocation of control rights

Aghion and Bolton (1992) propose a firm's capital structure as the allocation of control rights. Their model considers the more stringent friction than the CSV model does. Specifically, a financial contract cannot be contingent on a firm's cash flow realization. Unlike in the CSV environment, no auditing is available. Also, as in the PA model, the contract cannot be contingent on an action chosen by an agent. In this section, I introduce the slightly modified version of their model.

Under these frictions, a manager seeks funding I from an investor by selling the ownership π at $t = 0$ ($I > 0$). There are many investors, so all the bargaining power is at the hands of the manager—the investor is fine as long as she receives at least I in expectation. At $t = 1$, there is a realization of the condition of the economy $\theta \in \{\theta_g, \theta_b\}$. θ_g corresponds to the economic boom (good condition), whereas θ_b means the economic downturn (bad condition). At $t = 2$, there is a realization of cash flow $x \in \{0, 1\}$.

The firm's cash flow distribution depends on the condition of the economy and the control holder's action $a \in \{a_g, a_b\}$, such that $y_j^i = E[x|\theta = \theta_i, a = a_j]$. a_g corresponds to the growth strategy, such as merger and acquisitions, while a_b indicates the conservative decision, including layoffs and selling assets. After cash flow is realized, the investor gets πx in accordance with the contract. The manager receives $(1 - \pi)x + l$, where l is private benefits, *which cannot be shared with the investor*. The value of a firm is hence $x + l$. The value of private benefits also depends on the condition of the economy and the control holder's action. I define l_j^i as its value given condition θ_i and action a_j. Then, I set the following assumption: (1) the first-best action in θ_j is a_j: $y_j^j + l_j^j > y_i^j + l_i^j, \forall j, i \neq j$ and (2) investment is feasible: $P[\theta = \theta_g] \min \{y_g^g, y_b^g\} + P[\theta = \theta_b] \min \{y_g^b, y_b^b\} \geq I$. The first assumption is reasonable given that the growth strategy maximizes the value of a firm during the boom whereas the conservative strategy is better during the economic downturn. The second assumption implies that investment is feasible regardless of actions.

I first describe the frictionless case—π is contingent on the manager's action. Under this assumption, the manager maximizes his surplus by writing a contract that allows the investor's ownership depending on the manager's action. Then, the manager's objective function becomes

$$\max\nolimits_{\pi, \{A_g, A_b\}} \sum\nolimits_{i \in \{g,b\}} P[\theta = \theta_i]E[(1 - \pi)x + l|\theta = \theta_i, a = A_i]$$

s.t. $$\sum\nolimits_{i \in \{g,b\}} P[\theta = \theta_i]E[\pi x|\theta = \theta_i, a = A_i] \geq I. \qquad \text{[IR]}$$

If IR did not bind, there would be a chance of slightly lowering π and increasing the surplus of the manager. IR hence binds at the optimal contract, implying:

$$\pi = I / \sum_{i \in \{g,b\}} P[\theta = \theta_i]E[x|\theta = \theta_i, a = A_i].$$

Then, this optimization problem is reduced to

$$\max\nolimits_{\{A_g, A_b\}} \sum\nolimits_{i \in \{g,b\}} P[\theta = \theta_i]E[x + l|\theta = \theta_i, a = A_i] - I.$$

Because the manager's objective function differs from expected firm value just by constant, he chooses the first-best action. I thus claim the following:

- **Induced action without friction:** The first-best action is exclusively induced.

This result implies that the first-best action maximizes the manager's surplus in the absence of friction. Because the manager's surplus under binding IR is

$$\sum\nolimits_{i \in \{g,b\}} P[\theta = \theta_i]E[x + l|\theta = \theta_i, a = A_i^*] - I,$$

where A_i^* is induced action in condition i, it is maximized if and only if the first-best action is induced.

I set a couple of assumptions for further analysis:

- **Comonotonicity of private benefits:** I assume $l_j^j > l_i^j, \forall j, i \neq j$.
- **Comonotonicity of monetary benefits:** I assume $y_j^j > y_i^j, \forall j, i \neq j$.

The first assumption corresponds to the situation whereby the manager's private benefits comove with the firm's value. The second assumption corresponds to the situation whereby monetary benefits comove with the firm's value.

I now consider the contract under limited commitment. Specifically, I derive the equilibrium in which the manager maximizes his surplus by writing a contract that does not allow the investor's ownership to depend on induced actions at $t = 1$. Then, the manager's optimization problem is

$$\max_{\pi, \{A_g, A_b\}} \sum_{i \in \{g, b\}} P[\theta = \theta_i] E[(1 - \pi)x + l | \theta = \theta_i, a = A_i]$$

s.t. $\quad \sum_{i \in \{g, b\}} P[\theta = \theta_i] E[\pi x | \theta = \theta_i, a = A_i^*] \geq I.$ [IR]

Notice that IR binds at the optimal contract as reducing π always raises the manager's surplus. As π is not contingent on the manager's action, even if the manager promises to induce certain actions in advance, he may break up this promise when he finds better actions *ex post*. Then, as the investor's ownership cannot be changed, the investor may receive less than I on average. The investor anticipates this move and demands the ownership that satisfies her under the premise that the manager choose the strategy that is *ex post* optimal for him, which is an equilibrium action $\{A_g^*, A_b^*\}$. Specifically, the investor demands that

$$\pi = I / \sum_{i \in \{g, b\}} P[\theta = \theta_i] E[x | \theta = \theta_i, a = A_i^*].$$

Suppose private benefits are comonotonic. As $(1 - \pi)x + l = (1 - \pi)(x + l) + \pi l$,

$$\arg \max_{A_i} E[(1 - \pi)x + l | \theta = \theta_i, a = A_i] = \arg \max_{A_i} E[x + l | \theta = \theta_i, a = A_i], \forall i,$$

regardless of π. Then, the first-best action is uniquely induced.

Suppose private benefits are not comonotonic. Let me define $\bar{\pi}$ such that

$$\bar{\pi} = \sup \left\{ \delta \mid \begin{array}{l} \arg \max_{A_i} E[(1 - \pi)x + l | \theta = \theta_i, a = A_i] \\ = \arg \max_{A_i} E[x + l | \theta = \theta_i, a = A_i], \forall \pi \leq \delta, \forall i \end{array} \right\}.$$

$\bar{\pi}$ is the maximum of the investor's ownership at which the manager chooses the first-best action in every condition. Also, I define π_{FB} as the ownership required for the investor to participate under the belief that the manager chooses the first-best action. Then,

$$\pi_{FB} = I / \sum_{i \in \{g, b\}} P[\theta = \theta_i] y_i^i.$$

If $\pi_{FB} \leq \bar{\pi}$, the first-best action becomes the equilibrium action.

However, there may be another equilibrium action. For example, if the manager has private benefits, such as reputation and empire building, the growth strategy maximizes private benefits, regardless of the condition of the economy. Then, $l_g^g > l_b^g, l_b^b < l_g^b$. In this case, the manager can choose a_g in both conditions. Indeed, as private benefits are comonotonic in the good condition, the manager chooses the first-best action a_g in the good condition. To see why the manager can choose a_g in the bad condition, let us define $\bar{\pi}_b$ such that

$$\bar{\pi}_b = \sup \left\{ \delta \mid \begin{array}{l} \arg\max_{A_b} E[(1-\pi)x + l | \theta = \theta_b, a = A_b] \\ = \arg\max_{A_b} E[x + l | \theta = \theta_b, a = A_b], \forall \pi \le \delta \end{array} \right\}.$$

$\bar{\pi}_b$ is the threshold ownership of the investor such that the manager chooses a_g in the bad condition if the investor's ownership exceeds that level. Also, I define π_{SB} as the ownership required for the investor to participate under the belief that the manager chooses a_g in the bad condition. Then,

$$\pi_{SB} = I/(P[\theta = \theta_g]y_g^g + P[\theta = \theta_b]y_g^b).$$

If $\pi_{SB} \ge \bar{\pi}_b$, the second-best action $(A_g^* = A_b^* = a_g)$ is also an equilibrium action. Thus, if $\pi_{SB} \ge \bar{\pi}_b$ and $\pi_{FB} \le \bar{\pi}$, there are multiple equilibrium actions. As $\bar{\pi} = \bar{\pi}_b$ under $l_g^g > l_b^g$, there are multiple equilibrium actions if $\pi_{FB} \le \bar{\pi}_b \le \pi_{SB}$.

From the preceding argument, I claim following:

- **Induced action under limited commitment:** Under comonotonicity of private benefits, the first-best action is uniquely induced. Under noncomonotonicity of private benefits, the first-best action becomes an equilibrium action if $\pi_{FB} \le \bar{\pi}$. Under $l_g^g > l_b^g, l_b^b < l_g^b$, the second-best action becomes an equilibrium action if $\pi_{SB} \ge \bar{\pi}_b$, and hence, there are multiple equilibrium actions if $\pi_{FB} \le \bar{\pi}_b \le \pi_{SB}$.

The issue of multiple equilibria is the direct outcome of limited commitment. Depending on fluctuating belief about the manager's action, the equilibrium action differs. In the next setting, I seek the possibility of resolving this problem through capital structure choice, that is, the allocation of control rights.

I finally allow the manager to specify a control holder in each condition. Specifically, I derive the equilibrium in which the manager maximizes his surplus by writing the contract that does not allow the investor's ownership to depend on induced actions at $t = 1$ but specifies the control holder in each condition. Then, the manager's optimization problem is

$$\max_{\pi, \{A_g, A_b\}, \{H_g, H_b\}} \sum_{i \in \{g, b\}} P[\theta = \theta_i] E[(1 - \pi)x + l | \theta = \theta_i, a = A_i]$$

s.t.
$$\sum_{i \in \{g, b\}} P[\theta = \theta_i] E[\pi x | \theta = \theta_i, a = A_i^*] \ge I, \qquad \text{[IR]}$$

$$\forall i \in \{g, b\}, A_i \in \arg\max_A E[\pi x | \theta = \theta_i, a = A] \text{ if } H_i = \text{investor}. \qquad \text{[IC]}$$

Here, $\{H_g, H_b\}$ is the choice of specifying the control holder for each condition. IR binds at the optimal contract as reducing π always raises the manager's surplus. The manager is subject to IC if and only if the manager gives up control rights and the investor is a control holder. Because IC is an additional constraint for the manager, choosing H_i = manager is weakly

45

optimal for the manager. This observation immediately implies that the equilibrium in the previous setting is the equilibrium in the current setting as well. The manager is incentive-compatible with giving up control rights if and only if the manager's optimal action coincides with the investor's one.

Suppose monetary benefits are comonotonic:

$$\arg\max_{A_i} E[\pi x|\theta = \theta_i, a = A_i] = \arg\max_{A_i} E[x + l|\theta = \theta_i, a = A_i], \forall i.$$

Then, the first-best action also maximizes the expected surplus of the investor in each condition. If $\pi_{FB} \leq \bar{\pi}$, the manager is willing to choose the first-best action and incentive-compatible with giving up control rights to the investor in each condition.

Suppose the growth strategy maximizes private benefits, regardless of the condition of the economy, but the conservative policy maximizes monetary benefits, regardless of the condition of the economy. Then, $l_g^g > l_b^g, l_b^b < l_g^b, y_g^g < y_b^g, y_b^b > y_g^b$. Because agency conflicts often arise from opposing two goals, empire building and cash saving, this assumption seems relevant. In this case, monetary benefits are comonotonic in the bad condition, while private benefits are not. Then,

$$\arg\max_{A_b} E[\pi x|\theta = \theta_b, a = A_b] = \arg\max_{A_b} E[x + l|\theta = \theta_b, a = A_b],$$

suggesting that the investor is willing to choose a_b in the bad condition. If $\pi_{FB} \leq \bar{\pi}_b$, the manager is also willing to choose a_b in the bad condition. Then, giving up control rights in the bad condition is incentive-compatible as the manager anticipates the same outcome as the one under his own control.

Summarizing these arguments, I claim the following:

- **Control right allocation inducing the first-best action:** Under comonotonicity of private benefits, allocating control rights to the manager in both conditions becomes an equilibrium contract (equity without voting rights), exclusively inducing the first-best action. Under comonotonicity of monetary benefits, if $\pi_{FB} \leq \bar{\pi}$, allocating control rights to the investor in both conditions becomes an equilibrium contract (equity with voting rights), exclusively inducing the first-best action. Under $l_g^g > l_b^g, l_b^b < l_g^b, y_g^g < y_b^g, y_b^b > y_g^b$, if $\pi_{FB} \leq \bar{\pi}_b$, allocating control rights to the manager in the good condition and the investor in the bad condition (debt) becomes an equilibrium contract, exclusively inducing the first-best action. Under the same condition, if $\pi_{FB} \leq \bar{\pi}_b \leq \pi_{SB}$, allocating control rights to the manager in both conditions becomes an equilibrium contract that can induce both the first-best and second-best actions.

One interesting observation is that giving control rights to the manager does not necessarily maximize the manager's surplus. For example, when private benefits are not comonotonic due to empire building but monetary benefits are, the investor could demand very high ownership, anticipating the manager would choose the action that reduces monetary benefits (a_g in both conditions, for example). If the demanded ownership exceeds a certain threshold, the manager would indeed deviate from the first-best action. On the other hand, by giving up control rights, the manager can credibly commit to the first-best action and shift away from empire building. In this way, the financial contract works as a commitment device, maximizing the manager's surplus.

Overall, this model rationalizes the use of debt as a valuable commitment device. In the presence of unverifiable cash flows and actions, allocating control rights to the one with the right incentives maximizes firm value.

5.6 Discussion

In this section, I have seen many setups that rationalize the use of debt as the optimal financial contract. Under the PA model by Hölmstrom (1979) and Harris and Raviv (1979), if a manager is risk-neutral, it is optimal to impose every risk on the manager, inducing the debt-like constant payoff of an investor, as such a contract efficiently allocates the risk of a cash flow between the manager and the investor and ties the manager's compensation with the firm's performance, incentivizing the manager to exert effort. A flat payoff of an investor simultaneously induces optimal risk-sharing and mitigates managerial moral hazard. Innes (1990) extends the PA model by considering additional constraints: limited liability and monotonicity constraints. These additional constraints generate the need for regime-switching in the pay of an investor—up to a certain level of cash flow, the investor's payoff perfectly aligns with the cash flow. This regime-switching feature is also rationalized as the optimal contract in the presence of CSV as discussed by Townsend (1979) as well as Gale and Hellwig (1985). In the presence of auditing, giving every cash flow to an investor is optimal for a manager to satisfy the investor's participation constraint while minimizing auditing costs. In the absence of auditing, a manager's payoff has to be insensitive to the cash flow for him to report cash flow truthfully. Finally, in the situation in which neither cash flow nor a manager's action/effort is observable, the optimal financial contract specifies the allocation of control rights between a manager and an investor contingent on a signal about the state of an economy. Then, instead of controlling a manager's action through a performance-sensitive pay or direct monitoring, removing his power under a certain condition improves the value of a firm. This also rationalizes the regime-switching feature of a debt contract. Overall, these proposals suggest that a standard debt contract can be an optimal way of distributing a firm's cash flow and control rights between a manager and an investor under various settings.

In the next section, I discuss how debt can be an optimal way of financing projects from a different perspective. Specifically, I focus on the heterogeneity of a firm's quality in the capital market, which requires the firm to signal its quality when uninformed investors purchase the security of a firm. I claim a firm's capital structure works as a signaling device that helps a firm of high quality distinguish itself from the rest.

Notes

1 $\mathbb{R}^{++}$ is the set of positive real numbers.
2 This suggests that $F_a(\underline{x}, a) = 0, F_a(\bar{x}, a) = 0, F_{aa}(\underline{x}, a) = 0, F_{aa}(\bar{x}, a) = 0$.
3 Because the investor is able to observe managerial efforts, he is able to give huge penalties against deviation from the specified effort level.
4 Notice that $\int_{\underline{x}}^{\bar{x}} a(x)b'(x)dx = (a(x)b(x))\big|_{\underline{x}}^{\bar{x}} - \int_{\underline{x}}^{\bar{x}} a'(x)b(x)dx$ from integration by parts.
5 As discussed later, the MLRP implies FOSD, therefore assuming FOSD is redundant. However, for an expository purpose, I assume FOSD separately.

6 Relaxing IC is done in two steps. First, I change from the original IC to the first-order condition. Second, I change from the first-order condition to

$$\int_{\underline{x}}^{\bar{x}} u(w(x)) f_a(x, a) dx - 1 \geq 0.$$

7 Here, I introduce the model similar to Tirole (2006).

Bibliography

Aghion, P. and Bolton, P. (1992). An incomplete contracts approach to financial contracting. *Review of Economic Studies*, 59(3):473–94.

Gale, D. and Hellwig, M. (1985). Incentive-compatible debt contracts: The one-period problem. *Review of Economic Studies*, 52(4):647–63.

Harris, M. and Raviv, A. (1979). Optimal incentive contracts with imperfect information. *Journal of Economic Theory*, 20(2):231–59.

Hölmstrom, B. (1979). Moral hazard and observability. *Bell Journal of Economics*, 10(1):74–91.

Innes, R. (1990). Limited liability and incentive contracting with ex-ante action choices. *Journal of Economic Theory*, 52(1):45–67.

Myerson, R. B. (1979). Incentive compatibility and the bargaining problem. *Econometrica*, 47(1):61–73.

Rogerson, W. P. (1985). The first-order approach to principal-agent problems. *Econometrica*, 53 (6):1357–67.

Tirole, J. (2006). *The Theory of Corporate Finance*. Princeton University Press, Princeton.

Townsend, R. M. (1979). Optimal contracts and competitive markets with costly state verification. *Journal of Economic Theory*, 21(2):265–93.

6

ASYMMETRIC INFORMATION

6.1 Overview

In this chapter, I focus on the models of external finance in the presence of asymmetric information between entrepreneurs and investors. These models show corporate capital structure works as a signaling device. I ultimately argue that firms undertake a dynamic strategy of capital structure choice, considering their capital structure signals their qualities.

6.2 Underpricing in an initial public offering

One consistent finding is that the first-day return of an initial public offering (IPO) stock is positive on average. This finding implies that an offering price is often undervalued. Why is an IPO stock undervalued?

Rock (1986) explains this phenomenon based on the premise that IPO firms determine offering prices in the presence of both informed and uninformed ones without knowing the identity of investor type. In the model, a firm sells stocks to external investors at an offering price per share p. As the firm does not know the identity of an investor, it does not differentiate an offering price by investor type. The firm's cash flow $x \in [\underline{x}, 1]$ is stochastic, following the CDF $F(x)$, where $dF(x)/dx > 0, \forall x \in (\underline{x}, 1)$. The expected value of the cash flow is $\bar{x}$, where $\underline{x} < \bar{x} < 1$. There are $n + 1$ risk-neutral investors ($n \geq 2$). Among them, n investors are uninformed and one is informed. Each is willing to invest the value of k, where $k \leq \underline{x} < \bar{x} < nk$. Under this assumption, the total supply of funds exceeds the fair value, meaning that the IPO tends to be oversubscribed, if uninformed investors participate. Also, one informed investor can at most fund k, which is at most the least level of cash flow—the firm is willing to attract uninformed investors. The risk-free rate is zero, and there is no arbitrage opportunity for uninformed investors—their outside options yield zero expected return.

I start with the case in which only uninformed investors participate. Suppose $p = \bar{x}$. Then, uninformed investors are indifferent about their outside options and purchasing IPO stocks, satisfying their participation constraints. If $p > \bar{x}$, they would not participate in an IPO as the expected return is negative. The firm hence chooses $p = \bar{x}$. Under equal rationing, each receives $1/n$ fraction of ownership.

I next investigate the case in which n investors are uninformed and one is informed. The informed investor knows the realized cash flow x and participates in an IPO if $p < x$ and does not if $p \geq x$. Then, the shares of each uninformed investor $a^U(x)$ depend on cash flow x. Under equal rationing,

$$a^U(x) = \begin{cases} 1/(n+1) & \text{if } p < x \\ 1/n & \text{if } p \geq x \end{cases}. \tag{6.1}$$

This result is called the *winner's curse*. When an uninformed investor acquires more ownership, the stock is unprofitable. In turn, when an uninformed investor acquires less ownership, the stock is profitable. Then, the expected return to each uninformed investor $r^U(p)$ is characterized by

$$\begin{aligned} r^U(p) &= \int_{\underline{x}}^p a^U(x)(x-p)dF(x) + \int_p^1 a^U(x)(x-p)dF(x) \\ &= \int_{\underline{x}}^p \frac{x-p}{n}dF(x) + \int_p^1 \frac{x-p}{n+1}dF(x) \\ &= \int_{\underline{x}}^p \frac{x-p}{n}dF(x) + \int_p^1 \frac{x-p}{n}dF(x) - \int_p^1 \frac{x-p}{n}dF(x) + \int_p^1 \frac{x-p}{n+1}dF(x) \\ &= \frac{\bar{x}-p}{n} - \left(\int_p^1 \frac{x-p}{n}dF(x) - \int_p^1 \frac{x-p}{n+1}dF(x) \right) \\ &= \frac{\bar{x}-p}{n} - \int_p^1 \frac{x-p}{n(n+1)}dF(x). \end{aligned} \tag{6.2}$$

Because each of the uninformed investors has to be at least indifferent about purchasing an IPO stock and an outside option, setting the offering price such that $r^U(p) = 0$ is optimal for the firm that attracts funds from uninformed investors. This condition is equivalent to

$$p = \bar{x} - \int_p^1 \frac{x-p}{n+1}dF(x). \tag{6.3}$$

Notice that

$$\int_p^1 \frac{x-p}{n+1}dF(x) \geq 0.$$

This implies that $p \leq \bar{x}$. If $p = \bar{x}$, the following equation needs to hold:

$$\int_{\bar{x}}^1 \frac{x-\bar{x}}{n+1}dF(x) = 0.$$

But, as $dF(x)/dx > 0, \forall x \in (\underline{x}, 1)$ and $\underline{x} < \bar{x} < 1$, the left-hand side of the preceding equation is positive, which is a contradiction. Thus, $p < \bar{x}$. If $p \leq \underline{x}$, as $dF(x)/dx > 0, \forall x \in (\underline{x}, 1)$ and $\underline{x} < \bar{x} < 1$,

$$\begin{aligned} \int_p^1 \frac{x-p}{n+1}dF(x) &= \int_{\underline{x}}^1 \frac{x-p}{n+1}dF(x). \\ &< \int_{\underline{x}}^1 (x-p)dF(x) \\ &= \bar{x} - p. \end{aligned}$$

Then, the right-hand side of equation (6.3) is strictly greater than p, which is a contradiction. Thus, $\underline{x} < p < \bar{x}$.

If uninformed investors do not participate in an IPO, one informed investor participates. If one informed investor participates, the firm can raise at most k where $k \leq \underline{x}$. Therefore, attracting uninformed investors is optimal, because the firm can raise p where $p > k$. Despite the cost of underpricing, the firm is willing to attract uninformed investors.

In summary, I claim the following:

- **IPO underpricing:** If only uninformed investors participate in an IPO, the offering price is equal to $\bar{x}$. If both informed and uninformed investors participate in an IPO, the offering price is strictly less than $\bar{x}$—underpricing occurs.

This finding suggests that underpricing an IPO occurs in the presence of uninformed and informed investors. Because uninformed investors are subject to the winner's curse, they require the offering price to be lower than the fair value to offset this cost.

In this way, Rock (1986) highlights the cost of equity finance because of the asymmetry between informed and uninformed entities. In the next model, I consider how firms could avoid this problem by signaling their types to uninformed investors.

6.3 Signaling through retained ownership

Leland and Pyle (1977) develop the model in which IPO firms signal their types to uninformed investors through their retained ownership. There are two types of firms: g and b. Let t be the type of a firm ($t \in g,b$). Firm t's value is stochastic and characterized by $x_t = t + e$, where $e \sim N[0, \sigma^2]$, that is, a normal distribution with mean 0 and variance σ^2 ($\sigma > 0$). Then, the mean value of a firm matches the type of the firm. We assume $g > b$. At period 1, a risk-averse entrepreneur of firm t gives risk-neutral external investors take-it-or-leave-it offer: purchase of ownership $1 - \beta_t$ ($0 \leq \beta_t < 1$) for share price V_t. At period 2, the firm's value is realized. Entrepreneurs have certainty equivalence (CE) such that $CE(w) = E[w] - \frac{k}{2}Var[w]$ for wealth w. In period 1, external investors have access to the security that yields zero expected return in period 2, which is the outside option of these investors.

Such certainty equivalence is relevant under utility with constant absolute risk aversion (CARA). To see why, consider utility function with CARA k ($k > 0$) and wealth $w = E[w] + e$, so that $E[w]$ is the mean of w while σ^2 is the variance of w. Substituting e by σu, where u follows a standard normal distribution, its expected utility is

$$
\begin{aligned}
EU(w) &= \int_{-\infty}^{\infty} -(\exp(-k(E[w] + \sigma u))/k)\left(\exp(-u^2/2)/\sqrt{2\pi}\right)du \\
&= -(\exp(-kE[w])/k)\int_{-\infty}^{\infty}\left(\exp(-k\sigma u - u^2/2)/\sqrt{2\pi}\right)du \\
&= -(\exp(-kE[w])/k)\int_{-\infty}^{\infty}\left(\exp(k^2\sigma^2/2 - (u + k\sigma)^2/2)/\sqrt{2\pi}\right)du \\
&= -(\exp(-kE[w])\exp(k^2\sigma^2/2)/k)\int_{-\infty}^{\infty}\left(\underbrace{\exp(-(u + k\sigma)^2/2)/\sqrt{2\pi}}_{\text{PDF for } N[-k\sigma,1]}\right)du \\
&= -\exp(-kE[w])\exp(k^2\sigma^2/2)/k \\
&= -\exp(-k(E[w] - k\sigma^2/2))/k.
\end{aligned}
$$

This result suggests that the expected utility of w is the same as the utility of a certain wealth $E[w] - k\sigma^2/2$. Therefore, $CE(w) = E[w] - k\sigma^2/2$.

Under this preference, the entrepreneur of firm t aims to maximize the following by choosing (β_t, V_t):

$$CE(\beta_t x_t + (1 - \beta_t)V_t) = \beta_t t + (1 - \beta_t)V_t - \frac{k}{2}\beta_t^2\sigma^2.$$

First, I consider the case in which external investors can distinguish firm types. Then, as long as external investors do not make losses, they take the offer. Specifically, they take the offer if $V_t \le t$ for each t. The entrepreneur of firm t maximizes CE by setting $V_t = t$ and $\beta_t = 0$. This outcome is efficient risk-sharing, because risk-neutral external investors take all the risks whereas risk-averse entrepreneurs take no risk.

Second, I analyze the case in which external investors cannot distinguish firm types by themselves. I then consider firms, good firms in particular, try to distinguish themselves from the rest by retaining the level of ownership that is distinct from the rest's. To investigate this situation, I define the Perfect Bayesian Equilibrium (PBE) of a signaling game as the set of strategies and beliefs that satisfy the following:

1   Sequential rationality: entrepreneurs' strategies are optimal, given external investors' beliefs.
2   Belief consistency: external investors' beliefs are derived from entrepreneurs' choices of retained ownership and common prior beliefs using Bayes' rule, *wherever possible.*

Note that belief consistency is conditional on the availability of relevant information. If, for example, external investors assess the probability of facing a particular type based on the strategies never reached by any entrepreneur, they cannot rely on either entrepreneurs' strategies or priors. Then, Bayes' rule does not work. In this case, they can form arbitrary beliefs. On the other hand, if entrepreneurs with different types retain different levels of ownership, external investors can recognize the type of an entrepreneur when they observe the level of ownership retained by each entrepreneur. If every entrepreneur uses the same strategy, external investors use priors to infer the distribution of each type when they observe the common level of ownership retained by entrepreneurs. This equilibrium can be solved by the following steps:

1   Assign strategies to entrepreneurs.
2   Derive beliefs for external investors according to Bayes' rule. Set arbitrary beliefs if it is not possible.
3   Derive the external investors' best responses.
4   In view of the external investors' best responses and beliefs, check whether entrepreneurs want to deviate from the strategies I assigned. If not, I have found a PBE. If they want to deviate, this is not equilibrium. Return to step 1 and assign different strategies to entrepreneurs.

Following this algorithm, I solve a separating PBE of this signaling game in which entrepreneurs of firms with different types retain different levels of ownership—we are most interested in a separating equilibrium in which entrepreneurs use retained ownership as the signal of firm type.

Suppose $\beta_g < \beta_b$. Then, $\mu(t = g|\beta = \beta_g) = 1$, $\mu(t = b|\beta = \beta_b) = 1$, where $\mu(t = x|\beta = y)$ is the probability of type being equal to x given the retained ownership being equal to y. Given this belief, the most profitable pricing strategy accepted by external investors is $V_t = t$, $\forall t$. However, external investors also agree to take offers if the entrepreneur of firm b retains β_g and chooses to offer g per share. Notice that

$$\underbrace{CE(\beta_g x_b + (1 - \beta_g)g)}_{b \text{ chooses } (\beta_g, g)}$$

$$= \quad \beta_g b + (1 - \beta_g)g - k\beta_g^2\sigma^2/2$$

$$> \quad b - k\beta_b^2\sigma^2/2$$

$$= \quad \underbrace{CE(\beta_b x_b + (1 - \beta_b)b)}_{b \text{ chooses } (\beta_b, b)}.$$

Then, the entrepreneur of firm b profitably deviates by mimicking the strategy of firm g's entrepreneur. Thus, $\beta_g > \beta_b$ at a separating equilibrium.

Suppose $\beta_g > \beta_b > 0$. Then, $\mu(t = g|\beta = \beta_g) = 1$, $\mu(t = b|\beta = \beta_b) = 1$. The most profitable pricing strategy accepted by external investors is $V_t = t$, $\forall t$. Set $\mu(t = g|\beta = 0) = p$, $\mu(t = b|\beta = 0) = 1 - p$, where p is arbitrary value in $[0, 1]$. Then, they agree to take offers if the entrepreneur of firm b retains zero ownership and chooses to offer $pg + (1 - p)b$ per share. Notice that

$$\underbrace{CE(pg + (1 - p)b)}_{b \text{ chooses } (0, pg+(1-p)b)}$$

$$= \quad pg + (1 - p)b$$

$$> \quad b - k\beta_b^2\sigma^2/2$$

$$= \quad \underbrace{CE(\beta_b x_b + (1 - \beta_b)b)}_{b \text{ chooses } (\beta_b, b)}.$$

Then, the entrepreneur of firm b profitably deviates by choosing to retain no ownership. Thus, $\beta_b = 0$ at a separating equilibrium.

Suppose $\beta_g > \beta_b = 0$. Then, $\mu(t = g|\beta = \beta_g) = 1$, $\mu(t = b|\beta = \beta_b) = 1$. The most profitable pricing strategy accepted by external investors is $V_t = t$, $\forall t$. Set monotonic beliefs such that $\mu(t = g|\beta = x) = 1$, $\forall x \geq \beta_g$, $\mu(t = b|\beta = x) = 1$, $\forall x < \beta_g$. This is consistent, because I can set arbitrary beliefs when external investors face strategies that are not chosen by entrepreneurs.

I first check whether the entrepreneur of firm b has an incentive to deviate. For $\forall \beta \geq \beta_g$, the entrepreneur of firm b can offer at most g. Notice that

$$\underbrace{CE(\beta x_b + (1 - \beta)g)}_{b \text{ chooses } (\beta, g)} \leq \underbrace{CE(\beta_b x_b + (1 - \beta_b)b)}_{b \text{ chooses } (\beta_b, b)}$$

$$\Updownarrow$$

$$(1 - \beta)(g - b) \leq k\beta^2\sigma^2/2.$$

Because $k\beta^2\sigma^2/2 - (1-\beta)(g-b)$ is an increasing function if $\beta \geq 0$, $\forall \beta \geq \beta_g$, $k\beta^2\sigma^2/2 \geq (1-\beta)(g-b)$ is equivalent to

$$(1-\beta_g)(g-b) \leq k\beta_g^2\sigma^2/2. \tag{6.4}$$

Given the beliefs of external investors, there is no incentive for the entrepreneur of firm b to deviate to β where $\beta < \beta_g$, because the offering price can be at most b despite the utility loss from taking on additional risk—external investors would not switch their beliefs by this deviation. Therefore, inequality (6.4) becomes the exact condition for the entrepreneur of firm b not to deviate.

I next check whether the entrepreneur of firm g has an incentive to deviate. For $\forall \beta \geq \beta_g$, the entrepreneur of firm g can offer at most g. Therefore, there is no incentive to deviate above, because it just increases the risk that the entrepreneur has to take. It suffices to check whether the entrepreneur has an incentive to deviate below. For $\forall \beta < \beta_g$, the entrepreneur of firm g can offer at most b. Notice that

$$\underbrace{CE(\beta x_g + (1-\beta)b)}_{g \text{ chooses } (\beta, b)} \leq \underbrace{CE(\beta_g x_g + (1-\beta_g)g)}_{g \text{ chooses } (\beta_g, g)}$$

$$\Updownarrow$$

$$k(\beta_g^2 - \beta^2)\sigma^2/2 \leq (1-\beta)(g-b).$$

I note that $(1-\beta)(g-b) - k(\beta_g^2 - \beta^2)\sigma^2/2$ is a decreasing function if $\beta \leq (g-b)/k\sigma^2$. Also, $(1-\beta_g)(g-b) \geq 0$. Therefore, $\forall \beta < \beta_g$, $(1-\beta)(g-b) - k(\beta_g^2 - \beta^2)\sigma^2/2 \geq 0$ if $\beta_g \leq (g-b)/k\sigma^2$. $\beta_g \leq (g-b)/k\sigma^2$ if

$$g - b \geq k\sigma^2. \tag{6.5}$$

Hence, inequality (6.5) is sufficient for the entrepreneur of firm g not to deviate. Thus, if inequalities (6.4) and (6.5) are simultaneously satisfied, there is a separating equilibrium.[1] Because inequality (6.4) is equivalent to

$$\beta_g \geq \frac{-(g-b) + \sqrt{(g-b)^2 + 2k\sigma^2(g-b)}}{k\sigma^2},$$

there is a separating equilibrium under inequality (6.5) if the right-hand side of the previous inequality is strictly less than 1. In fact, the right-hand side of that inequality is strictly less than 1, because

$$1 - \left(-(g-b) + \sqrt{(g-b)^2 + 2k\sigma^2(g-b)}\right)/k\sigma^2$$

$$= \left((g-b) + k\sigma^2 - \sqrt{(g-b)^2 + 2k\sigma^2(g-b)}\right)/k\sigma^2$$

$$= \left(\sqrt{((g-b) + k\sigma^2)^2} - \sqrt{(g-b)^2 + 2k\sigma^2(g-b)}\right)/k\sigma^2$$

$$= \left(\sqrt{(g-b)^2 + 2k\sigma^2(g-b) + k^2\sigma^4} - \sqrt{(g-b)^2 + 2k\sigma^2(g-b)}\right)/k\sigma^2$$

$$> 0.$$

Thus, I claim the following:

- **Signaling through retained ownership:** Suppose $k\sigma^2 \le g - b$. There is a separating equilibrium in which $V_t = t, \forall t, \beta_b = 0, (1 - \beta_g)(g - b) \le k\beta_g^2\sigma^2/2$.

The parametric assumption I imposed in this proposition means that the quality difference between the two types of firms is large compared to the utility loss from risk-taking so that firm g has an incentive to distinguish itself from firm b by taking on risk.

Compared to the case in which investors recognize firm types, firm g needs to retain some ownership at a separating equilibrium. This is the utility loss for firm g's entrepreneur, who is risk-averse. I can interpret such utility loss as a signaling cost to distinguish firm g from firm b.

Because this cost is a deadweight loss for society, the most efficient equilibrium among the set of separating equilibira is the one with the least ownership retained by firm g's entrepreneur. Such β_g is characterized by

$$\beta_g = \frac{-(g - b) + \sqrt{(g - b)^2 + 2k\sigma^2(g - b)}}{k\sigma^2}. \tag{6.6}$$

6.4 Signaling through debt

Ross (1977) develops the model whereby firms signal their types to uninformed investors through debt. There are two types of firms: g and b. The firm with type t (firm t) has a constant value characterized by t. Firm t sells $(1 - \beta)$ ownership to uninformed external investors and offers V_t per share.

Unlike in the previous model, firms do not differentiate their retained ownership, so both firms choose to retain β $(0 < \beta < 1)$, which is exogenously determined. This model, rather, allows firms to choose different levels of debt to signal their types. Let us denote the level of debt chosen by firm t by D_t, where $D_t \in \{l, h\}$ and $l \le b < h \le g$.

Under this setting, the surplus of firm t, U_t, depends on the relative balance of firm value t and debt level D_t. If debt is excessive relative to firm value, the surplus of the firm falls, owing to the cost of financial distress incurred by a firm's manager. Specifically, it is defined by

$$U_t = \begin{cases} (1 - \beta)V_t + \beta t & \text{if } D_t \le t \\ (1 - \beta)V_t + \beta(t - d) & \text{if } D_t > t \end{cases},$$

where d is *managerial* default cost, such as a search cost for a new job. Firm t maximizes U_t by optimally choosing (D_t, V_t) in the signaling game. Here, I use the same definition of PBE except that external investors' beliefs are derived from the firms' choices of debt instead of retained ownership. In accordance with this change, external investors have a belief function $\mu(t = x|D = y)$, which is the probability of type being equal to x given the debt equal to y. Following the algorithm in the previous section, I solve a separating PBE of this signaling game.

Suppose $D_g = l < h = D_b$. Then, $\mu(t = g|D = D_g) = 1$, $\mu(t = b|D = D_b) = 1$. The most profitable pricing strategy accepted by external investors is $V_t = t, \forall t$. However, external investors also agree to take offers if firm b raises D_g and chooses to offer g per share. Notice that

$$\underbrace{(1 - \beta)g + \beta b}_{b \text{ chooses } (D_g, g)} > \underbrace{(1 - \beta)b + \beta(b - d)}_{b \text{ chooses } (D_b, b)}.$$

Then, firm b profitably deviates by choosing D_g. Thus, $D_g > D_b$ at a separating equilibrium. Suppose $D_g = h > l = D_b$. Then, $\mu(t = g | D = D_g) = 1$, $\mu(t = b | D = D_b) = 1$. The most profitable pricing strategy accepted by external investors is $V_t = t$, $\forall t$. However, external investors also agree to take offers if firm b raises D_g and chooses to offer g per share. Notice that

$$\underbrace{(1 - \beta)g + \beta(b - d)}_{b \text{ chooses } (D_g, g)} \leq \underbrace{(1 - \beta)b + \beta b}_{b \text{ chooses } (D_b, b)}$$

$$\Updownarrow$$

$$(1 - \beta)(g - b) \leq \beta d. \tag{6.7}$$

Then, if inequality (6.7) is satisfied, there is no incentive for firm b to deviate. In turn, external investors agree to take offers if firm g raises D_b and chooses to offer b per share. However, there is no incentive to do so, because

$$\underbrace{(1 - \beta)b + \beta g}_{g \text{ chooses } (D_b, b)} \leq g$$

$$= \underbrace{(1 - \beta)g + \beta g}_{g \text{ chooses } (D_g, g)}.$$

Thus, inequality (6.7) is sufficient for the presence of a separating equilibrium.
I thus claim the following:

- **Signaling through debt:** Suppose $(1 - \beta)(g - b) \leq \beta d$. There is a separating equilibrium in which $V_t = t$, $\forall t$, $D_b = l < h = D_g$.

The parametric assumption I imposed in this proposition means that the value gain from mimicking a good firm is small compared to managerial loss from default. Then, firm b does not have an incentive to deviate above.

Overall, this model suggests that the amount of raised debt is positively correlated with firm quality. This result is consistent with the finding from the earlier model—the amount of equity issuance is negatively correlated with firm quality. As discussed in the next section, Myers and Majluf (1984) integrated both ideas into one capital structure theory.

6.5 Pecking-order versus trade-off theory

The previous three models show the cost of raising funds from uninformed investors and rationalize the use of retained ownership and debt as a signal of a high-quality firm. These models suggest that firms in good conditions should start by using internal funds to avoid any cost from raising funds from uninformed investors. Then, if internal financing is difficult, firms should prioritize debt over equity, as retaining ownership and raising high debt signals good firm quality. If their conditions become worse, they can use equity as a last resort. This hypothesis motivates the *pecking-order* of dynamic capital structure choice. Myers and Majluf (1984) develop the theory of dynamic capital structure choice in accordance with this premise—firms first use internal funds to avoid external finance, second choose debt, and finally raise equity.

For the rest of this section, I briefly summarize the empirical findings about corporate capital structure that are related to the pecking-order theory, following Frank and Goyal (2007).

First, there is empirical evidence that leverage and profitability are negatively correlated, as argued by Titman and Wessels (1988) and Kayhana and Titman (2007). Considering profitability is negatively associated with bankruptcy cost, the trade-off theory predicts the positive correlation between profitability and leverage. The trade-off theory is hence inconsistent with this result. On the other hand, the pecking-order theory is consistent with this fact, because it predicts firms prefer internal finance over external finance, including debt, when firms are profitable.

Second, leverage and growth opportunities are negatively correlated. In particular, Rajan and Zingales (1995) show the negative relation between market-to-book ratios and leverage, which are proxies for firms' growth opportunities, exists in all G7 countries. Considering growth firms lose more of their value when they go into distress, they tend to have larger bankruptcy costs. The trade-off theory predicts growth firms use less debt. The trade-off theory is hence consistent with this empirical fact. By contrast, the pecking-order theory predicts firms with more investments—holding profitability fixed—should accumulate more debt over time. The pecking-order theory predicts growth opportunities and leverage are expected to be positively related. Thus, the pecking-order theory is inconsistent with this fact.

Overall, there is mixed evidence for the pecking-order theory against the trade-off theory. On one hand, the pecking-order theory is consistent with the negative correlation between profitability and leverage, whereas the trade-off theory cannot explain this pattern. On the other hand, the trade-off theory is consistent with the negative correlation between growth opportunities and leverage, whereas the pecking-order theory cannot explain this relation.

6.6 Discussion

The pecking-order theory, based on the presence of asymmetric information among stakeholders, has been the major competing theory against the trade-off theory. Indeed, the pecking-order theory explains some of the empirical facts that cannot be explained by the trade-off theory. However, it poses some puzzles as well.

One major issue is, as discussed earlier, that the pecking-order theory (at least its static version) cannot explain the negative correlation between market-to-book ratios and leverage. Indeed, if the pecking-order theory is valid, periods of high investment opportunities, which are measured by market-to-book ratios, should push leverage higher. Baker and Wurgler (2002) respond to this issue by proposing a new theory of capital structure: the *market-timing* theory. This theory rather suggests that capital structure is the cumulative outcome of attempts to time the equity market (Baker and Wurgler, 2002). In their interpretation, market-to-book ratios capture firms' overvaluation rather than investment opportunities. The negative correlation between market-to-book ratios and leverage reflects the simple strategy of a firm issuing equity when they are overvalued (high market-to-book ratios) and repurchasing when they are undervalued (low market-to-book ratios). Dong et al. (2012) provide empirical evidence that is consistent with the market-timing theory.

Note

1 Note that inequality (6.5) is sufficient for the entrepreneur of firm g not to deviate. The exact condition is different from inequality (6.5).

Bibliography

Baker, M. and Wurgler, J. (2002). Market timing and capital structure. *Journal of Finance*, 57 (1):1–32.

Dong, M., Hirshleifer, D., and Teoh, S. H. (2012). Overvalued equity and financing decisions. *Review of Financial Studies*, 25(12):3645–83.

Frank, M. Z. and Goyal, V. K. (2007). Trade-off and pecking order theories of debt. In Eckbo, E., editor, *Empirical Corporate Finance, Volume 2 of Handbook of Corporate Finance*, Chapter 12, pages 135–202. Elsevier, Amsterdam.

Kayhana, A. and Titman, S. (2007). Firms' histories and their capital structures. *Journal of Financial Economics*, 83(1):1–32.

Leland, H. E. and Pyle, D. H. (1977). Informational asymmetries, financial structure, and financial intermediation. *Journal of Finance*, 32(2):371–87.

Myers, S. C. and Majluf, N. S. (1984). Corporate financing and investment decisions when firms have information that investors do not have. *Journal of Financial Economics*, 13(2):187–221.

Rajan, R. G. and Zingales, L. (1995). What do we know about capital structure? some evidence from international data. *Journal of Finance*, 50(5):1421–60.

Rock, K. (1986). Why new issues are underpriced? *Journal of Financial Economics*, 15(1–2):187–212.

Ross, S. A. (1977). The determination of financial structure: The incentive-signalling approach. *Bell Journal of Economics*, 8(1):23–40.

Titman, S. and Wessels, R. (1988). The determinants of capital structure choice. *Journal of Finance*, 43(1):1–19.

7

CONTINUOUS-TIME MODEL

7.1 Overview

In this chapter, we utilize a derivative valuation model to simulate the realistic valuation of equity and debt. Then, we update traditional frameworks covered in earlier chapters. First, I cover Merton (1974) and derive the irrelevance of capital structure as in Chapter 2. Second, I review Leland (1994), which is the quantitative version of the static trade-off theory covered in Chapter 3, and show that firms determine their capital structure by trading off bankruptcy costs and the tax benefit of debt.

7.2 Derivative valuation model

In quantitative finance, every security, including equity and debt, is considered a derivative of a firm's asset. It is traded in the same market where a risk-free debt is traded. Then, I measure its value by considering its instantaneous expected return *after adjusting its risk* is equal to the risk-free rate so that investors cannot arbitrate securities. This condition is eventually characterized by a partial differential equation. The solution of the equation becomes its value.

Before modeling derivative pricing, I briefly review a Brownian motion Z. A Brownian motion is a limit of random walk. Specifically, a change in the motion from time t to $t + x$, where $x \geq 0$, satisfies

$$Z_{t+x} - Z_t \sim N[0, x], \text{ which is a normal distribution with mean } 0 \text{ and variance } x.$$

Here, an instantaneous change in Brownian motion dZ, which is defined as $Z_{t+dt} - Z_t$, follows normal distribution with mean 0 and variance dt. Each change is identically and independently distributed. Because the move of Z is considered the sum of these small changes, it is describable in the form of an integral. The integral of dZ from t to T is

$$\begin{aligned}
\int_t^T dZ &= Z_T - Z_t \\
&= Z_{t+T-t} - Z_t \\
&\sim N[0, T - t].
\end{aligned}$$

Suppose a firm's asset value at time t, A_t, follows a geometric Brownian motion. This means that

$$dA_t = \mu A_t dt + \sigma A_t dZ. \tag{7.1}$$

This characterization reflects an instantaneous percent change in the value of a firm's asset is random, and its mean and standard deviation are constant at any t. μ is called the percentage drift while σ is called the percentage volatility ($\sigma > 0$).

Let us denote the kth security price be $f_k(A_t, t)$, which is a function of a firm's asset value A_t and time t. f_k is considered a derivative of a firm's asset. I then would like to derive an instantaneous change in f_k. A Taylor expansion around $f_k(A_t, t)$ suggests that an instantaneous change in f_k, df_k, is

$$df_k = \frac{\partial f_k}{\partial A_t} dA_t + \frac{1}{2}\frac{\partial^2 f_k}{\partial A_t^2} dA_t^2 + \frac{\partial f_k}{\partial t} dt + \frac{1}{2}\frac{\partial^2 f_k}{\partial t^2} dt^2.$$

Let us closely look at dA_t^2. Equation (7.1) suggests that

$$dA_t^2 = \mu^2 A_t^2 dt^2 + 2\mu\sigma A_t^2 dt dZ + \sigma^2 A_t^2 dZ^2,$$

where

$$dt dZ \sim dt N[0, dt],$$
$$dZ^2 \sim d_t \chi_1^2.$$

Here, χ_1^2 stands for a chi-squared distribution with 1 degree of freedom. In Ito's calculus, which is the benchmark mathematics in this field, a random variable is a scalar equal to its mean if its variance is an infinitesimal of higher order than dt, which is a variance of dZ. The variance of $dt dZ$ is dt^3 while the variance of dZ^2 is $2dt^2$. Both are hence scalars equal to their means 0 and dt, respectively. Because dt^2 is zero as in usual calculus,

$$dA_t^2 = \sigma^2 A_t^2 dt.$$

Because dt^2 is zero,

$$df_k = \left(\frac{\partial f_k}{\partial t} + \frac{\partial f_k}{\partial A_t}\mu A_t + \frac{1}{2}\frac{\partial^2 f_k}{\partial A_t^2}\sigma^2 A_t^2 \right) dt + \frac{\partial f_k}{\partial A_t}\sigma A_t dZ.$$

This is called Ito's lemma. Let us denote the kth security's coupon to be $c_k(A_t, t)$. The total return of f_k is

$$\frac{c_k dt + df_k}{f_k} = \left(\frac{\partial f_k}{\partial t} + \frac{\partial f_k}{\partial A_t}\mu A_t + \frac{1}{2}\frac{\partial^2 f_k}{\partial A_t^2}\sigma^2 A_t^2 + c_k \right) dt/f_k + \frac{\partial f_k}{\partial A_t}\sigma A_t dZ/f_k.$$

Suppose there is a portfolio consisting of A_t itself (f_1) and an arbitrary security (f_k). The two securities' weights are $\{w, 1-w\}$. The portfolio's total return is

$$w\frac{(\mu A_t dt + \sigma A_t dZ)}{A_t} + (1-w)\frac{c_k dt + df_k}{f_k},$$

which is equivalent to

$$\left(w\mu + \frac{1-w}{f_k}\left(\frac{\partial f_k}{\partial t} + \frac{\partial f_k}{\partial A_t}\mu A_t + \frac{1}{2}\frac{\partial^2 f_k}{\partial A_t^2}\sigma^2 A_t^2 + c_k\right)\right)dt + \left(w + \frac{1-w}{f_k}\frac{\partial f_k}{\partial A_t}A_t\right)\sigma dZ.$$

If $w + (1-w)(\partial f_k/\partial A_t)A_t/f_k = 0$, the portfolio becomes risk-free. Then, it needs to be equal to the risk-free rate rdt in the absence of arbitrage opportunities ($r > 0$). Thus, the following equivalent conditions need to be satisfied:

$$\left(w\mu + \frac{1-w}{f_k}\left(\frac{\partial f_k}{\partial t} + \frac{\partial f_k}{\partial A_t}\mu A_t + \frac{1}{2}\frac{\partial^2 f_k}{\partial A_t^2}\sigma^2 A_t^2 + c_k\right)\right)dt = rdt$$

$$w(\mu - r) + \frac{1-w}{f_k}\left(\frac{\partial f_k}{\partial t} + \frac{\partial f_k}{\partial A_t}\mu A_t + \frac{1}{2}\frac{\partial^2 f_k}{\partial A_t^2}\sigma^2 A_t^2 + c_k - rf_k\right) = 0$$

$$-(1-w)\frac{\partial f_k}{\partial A_t}\frac{A_t(\mu - r)}{f_k} + \frac{1-w}{f_k}\left(\frac{\partial f_k}{\partial t} + \frac{\partial f_k}{\partial A_t}\mu A_t + \frac{1}{2}\frac{\partial^2 f_k}{\partial A_t^2}\sigma^2 A_t^2 + c_k - rf_k\right) = 0$$

$$\frac{\partial f_k}{\partial A_t}A_t(r - \mu) + \frac{\partial f_k}{\partial t} + \frac{\partial f_k}{\partial A_t}\mu A_t + \frac{1}{2}\frac{\partial^2 f_k}{\partial A_t^2}\sigma^2 A_t^2 + c_k - rf_k = 0.$$

Thus, f_k satisfies the following equation:

$$\frac{\partial f_k}{\partial t} + \frac{\partial f_k}{\partial A_t}rA_t + \frac{1}{2}\frac{\partial^2 f_k}{\partial A_t^2}\sigma^2 A_t^2 - rf_k + c_k = 0. \tag{7.2}$$

In summary, I claim the following:

- **Derivative pricing equation:** Under the no-arbitrage condition, an arbitrary security price, f_k, satisfies the partial differential equation (7.2) if it is traded in the same market in which a risk-free debt and a firm's asset are traded.

Importantly, equation (7.2) suggests that f_k does not depend on the percentage drift term μ for the process of a firm's asset value. In accordance with this result, the solution to this equation does not depend on μ. Because a firm's asset does not yield any coupon, its instantaneous expected return after adjusting its risk becomes the risk-free rate under the no-arbitrage condition. Its derivative's risk-adjusted instantaneous expected return only depends on an underlying asset's risk-adjusted instantaneous expected return (risk-free rate).

The solution to this equation is called the Feynman–Kac equation. In particular, it is represented as the expected sum of discounted future claims under some probability measure where the discount rate is the risk-free rate. To see how intuitively, I first derive it in the context of the Arrow–Debreu model in Chapter 2. Recall that in the Arrow–Debreu model, where there are J states, the vector of security prices V satisfies

$$V = \sum_{j=1}^{J}\Gamma_j\psi_j = \Gamma\psi,$$

where Γ is a payoff matrix and ψ is the state price vector. Because the risk-free rate r is defined as how much the price of a safe security that yields 1 in every state is dicounted relative to its face value 1, the risk-free rate is derived by

$$(1+r)^{-1} = \sum_{j=1}^{J} \psi_j.$$

Then,

$$
\begin{aligned}
V &= \sum_{j=1}^{J} \Gamma_j \psi_j \\
&= \sum_{j=1}^{J} \psi_j \sum_{j=1}^{J} \Gamma_j \psi_j / \sum_{j=1}^{J} \psi_j \\
&= (1+r)^{-1} \sum_{j=1}^{J} \Gamma_j \pi_j \\
&= (1+r)^{-1} \Gamma \pi.
\end{aligned}
\tag{7.3}
$$

where π is a vector with its element $\pi_j = \psi_j / \sum_{j=1}^{J} \psi_j$. Notice that $\sum_{j=1}^{J} \pi_j = 1$. Recall also $\pi_j > 0$, $\forall j$, under the no-arbitrage condition as discussed in Chapter 2. Therefore, π is a valid probability measure. Equation (7.3) suggests that a vector of security prices is the expected sum of discounted future claims under π where the discount rate is r. I call such a probability measure a *risk-neutral* measure.

I now show that the earlier idea in the Arrow–Debreu model can be applied to our current setting. I start by investigating the associated process Y_s ($s \geq t$) defined as

$$Y_s = \exp\left(-\int_t^s r\,dl\right) f_k(A_s^Q, s) + \int_t^s \exp\left(-\int_t^s r\,d\eta\right) c_k(A_l^Q, l)\,dl,$$

where

$$
\begin{aligned}
dA_s^Q &= rA_s^Q dt + \sigma A_s^Q dZ, \\
A_t^Q &= A_t.
\end{aligned}
\tag{7.4}
$$

An instantaneous return defined by equation (7.4) is a risk-adjusted version of an instantaneous return defined by equation (7.1). Indeed, the instantaneous expected return suggested by equation (7.4) is r, which matches the risk-adjusted instantaneous expected return of a firm's asset. Using a product rule,

$$
\begin{aligned}
dY_s &= \exp\left(-\int_t^s r\,dl\right) df_k - r\exp\left(-\int_t^s r\,dl\right) f_k ds \\
&\quad \underbrace{-r\exp\left(-\int_t^s r\,dl\right) ds df_k}_{=\,0 \text{ because } dsdZ=0} + \exp\left(-\int_t^s r\,d\eta\right) c_k ds \\
&= \exp\left(-\int_t^s r\,dl\right)(df_k - rf_k ds + c_k ds) \\
&= \exp\left(-\int_t^s r\,dl\right)\left(\frac{\partial f_k}{\partial s} + \frac{\partial f_k}{\partial A_k^Q} rA_k^Q + \frac{1}{2}\frac{\partial f_k^2}{\partial A_s^{Q2}}\sigma^2 A_k^{Q2} - rf_k + c_k\right) ds \\
&\quad + \exp\left(-\int_t^s r\,dl\right)\frac{\partial f_k}{\partial A_s^Q}\sigma A_s^Q dZ.
\end{aligned}
$$

Suppose f_k is a solution to equation (7.2):

$$dY_s = \exp\left(-\int_t^s rdl\right)\frac{\partial f_k}{\partial A_s^Q}\sigma A_s^Q dZ.$$

Notice that this follows a normal distribution with a mean of 0. Then,

$$
\begin{aligned}
Y_T - Y_t &= \int_t^T dY_s \\
&= \int_t^T \exp\left(-\int_t^s rdl\right)\frac{\partial f_k}{\partial A_s^Q}\sigma A_s^Q dZ
\end{aligned}
$$

has a mean of zero as it is the sum of normal distributions with a mean of 0. Such a property is called a *martingale*:

$$E_t[Y_T - Y_t] = 0,$$

where I use an operator E_t to indicate the expectation at time t. Hence,

$$
\begin{aligned}
f_k &= Y_t \\
&= E_t[Y_t] \\
&= E_t[Y_T] \\
&= E_t\left[\exp\left(-\int_t^T rdl\right)\underbrace{f_k(A_T^Q, T)}_{\text{terminal value}} + \int_t^T \exp\left(-\int_t^l rd\eta\right)c_k(A_l^Q, l)dl\right].
\end{aligned}
\tag{7.5}
$$

In summary, I claim the following:

- **Solution for derivative pricing equation:** The solution to the partial differential equation (7.2) is equation (7.5).

Importantly, equation (7.5) suggests that f_k is the expected sum of discounted future claims under the condition that an underlying asset value follows a stochastic process $\{A_s^Q\}_{s\geq t}$ with the discount rate r, that is, the risk-free rate. Again, a security price is the expected sum of discounted future claims under some probability measure (risk-neutral measure). Under this measure, a firm's asset value follows the process defined by equation (7.4).

This formula is computable if the terminal value function and the coupon function are known. Undertaking a Monte Carlo simulation and taking the average, equation (7.5) is numerically solvable.

7.3 Capital structure irrelevance revisited

Using the derivative valuation model, Merton (1974) evaluates a firm's equity and debt and derives capital structure irrelevance, which I covered in Chapter 2. His model is a pure asset-pricing model in the sense that the process of generating asset value is ignored. A firm is a machine whose asset value varies due to exogenous shocks. Its debt holder receives face value M at the maturity of debt T without coupons ($M > 0$). Its equity holder receives zero dividends. At the maturity of debt T, he sells the firm's asset in order to repay debt.

Table 7.1 Summary of Payoffs

State	Debt	Equity
$A_T < M$	A_T	0
$A_T \geq M$	M	$A_T - M$

If there is a remaining value, he earns it. If the firm's asset value at maturity is below the face value of debt, the firm defaults and its debt holder instead owns the firm's asset whereas its equity holder receives none. Table 7.1 summarizes the payoffs of securities at maturity.

Merton (1974) considers a firm's equity holder a buyer of a European call option of a firm's asset with a strike price equal to the face value of debt M. The maturity of the option matches the maturity of debt T. Like a buyer of a call option when buying at a strike price is unprofitable ($M > A_T$), an equity holder receives none at maturity, as if the buyer of an option does not exercise it. As the buyer of an option when buying at a strike price is profitable ($A_T \geq M$), an equity holder receives $A_T - M$ at maturity, as if the buyer of an option exercises it. From this analogy, my conjecture is that the Black–Scholes model, usually used for option pricing, is applicable to the price of equity. In the next paragraph, I verify this conjecture using the Feynman–Kac equation. Let us denote the price of equity at time t by $S(A_t, t)$, where $t \leq T$.

Based on our setting, the terminal value of equity is defined as follows.

$$S(A_T, T) = \max\{A_T - M, 0\}.$$

Because there is no dividend, equation (7.5) suggests that

$$S(A_t, t) = E_t\left[\exp\left(-\int_t^T rdl\right)S(A_T^Q, T)\right]$$

$$= \exp(-r(T-t))E_t\left[\max\{A_T^Q - M, 0\}\right].$$

Using Ito's lemma, I know that

$$d\ln(A_s^Q) = \left(\frac{1}{A_s^Q}rA_s^Q - \frac{1}{2}\frac{1}{A_s^{Q2}}\sigma^2 A_s^{Q2}\right)ds + \frac{1}{A_s^Q}\sigma A_s^Q dZ$$

$$= \left(r - \frac{\sigma^2}{2}\right)ds + \sigma dZ.$$

Therefore,

$$\ln(A_T^Q) - \ln(A_t) = \ln(A_T^Q) - \ln(A_t^Q)$$

$$= \int_t^T d\ln(A_s^Q)$$

$$= \underbrace{\int_t^T\left(r - \frac{\sigma^2}{2}\right)ds}_{\text{constant}} + \underbrace{\int_t^T \sigma dZ}_{N[0,\sigma^2(T-t)]}.$$

$$\sim N\left[\left(r - \frac{\sigma^2}{2}\right)(T-t), \sigma^2(T-t)\right].$$

Hence,

$$\ln\left(A_T^Q\right) \sim N\left[\ln\left(A_t\right) + \left(r - \frac{\sigma^2}{2}\right)(T-t), \sigma^2(T-t)\right].$$

For convenience, I define two parameters:

$$d_1 = \frac{\ln\left(A_t/M\right) + (r+\sigma^2/2)(T-t)}{\sigma\sqrt{T-t}},$$

$$d_2 = \frac{\ln\left(A_t/M\right) + (r-\sigma^2/2)(T-t)}{\sigma\sqrt{T-t}}.$$

Denoting the PDF and CDF of a standard normal distribution by ϕ and Φ,

$$
\begin{aligned}
E_t\left[\max\{A_T^Q - M, 0\}\right] &= \int_{\ln(M)}^{\infty} \frac{\exp(s) - M}{\sigma\sqrt{T-t}}\phi\left(\frac{s - (\ln(A_t) + (r - \sigma^2/2)(T-t))}{\sigma\sqrt{T-t}}\right)ds \\
&= \int_{\ln(M)}^{\infty} \frac{\exp(s)}{\sigma\sqrt{T-t}}\phi\left(\frac{s - (\ln(A_t) + (r - \sigma^2/2)(T-t))}{\sigma\sqrt{T-t}}\right)ds \\
&\quad - M(1 - \Phi(-d_2)) \\
&= \int_{-d_2}^{\infty} \exp\left(\sigma\sqrt{T-t}\,z + \ln(A_t) + \left(r - \frac{\sigma^2}{2}\right)(T-t)\right)\phi(z)dz \\
&\quad - M\Phi(d_2) \\
&= \exp\left(\ln(A_t) + \left(r - \frac{\sigma^2}{2}\right)(T-t)\right) \\
&\quad \times \int_{-d_2}^{\infty} \exp(\sigma\sqrt{T-t}\,z)\phi(z)dz - M\Phi(d_2) \\
&= \exp\left(\ln(A_t) + \left(r - \frac{\sigma^2}{2}\right)(T-t)\right)\exp\left(\frac{\sigma^2}{2}(T-t)\right) \\
&\quad \times \int_{-d_2}^{\infty} \phi\left(z - \sigma\sqrt{T-t}\right)dz - M\Phi(d_2) \\
&= \exp(r(T-t))A_t(1 - \Phi(-d_2 - \sigma\sqrt{T-t})) - M\Phi(d_2) \\
&= \exp(r(T-t))A_t\Phi(d_1) - M\Phi(d_2).
\end{aligned}
$$

From this observation,

$$
\begin{aligned}
S(A_t, t) &= \exp(-r(T-t))E_t\left[\max\{A_T^Q - M, 0\}\right] \\
&= A_t\Phi(d_1) - \exp(-r(T-t))M\Phi(d_2).
\end{aligned}
\tag{7.6}
$$

In turn, Merton (1974) considers a firm's debt a portfolio of safe security and short European put option. Safe security returns M for sure at maturity T. The European put option corresponds to the European call option discussed earlier. The maturity of the option is the maturity of debt T and the strike price is M. When selling at a strike price is unprofitable at maturity ($A_T \geq M$), the buyer of the put option receives none as he does not exercise an option. When selling at a strike price is profitable at maturity ($M > A_T$), he receives $M - A_T$ as he exercises an option. In turn, when $A_T \geq M$, the seller of the put option receives none, as the option is not exercised. When $M > A_T$, the seller countertrades and earns $A_T - M$, as the option is exercised. Hence, indeed, the portfolio return matches the payoff of debt: M when $A_T \geq M$ and A_T when $M > A_T$. Let us denote the price of debt by $B(A_t, t)$.

Like the terminal value of equity, that of debt is defined as follows:

$$B(A_T, T) = \min\{A_T, M\}.$$

Because there is no coupon, equation (7.5) suggests that

$$
\begin{aligned}
B(A_t, t) &= E_t\left[\exp\left(-\int_t^T r\,dl\right)B(A_T^Q, T)\right] \\
&= \exp(-r(T-t))E_t\left[\min\{A_T^Q, M\}\right] \\
&= \exp(-r(T-t))E_t\left[A_T^Q - \max\{A_T^Q - M, 0\}\right] \\
&= \exp(-r(T-t))E_t\left[A_T^Q\right] - \exp(-r(T-t))E_t\left[\max\{A_T^Q - M, 0\}\right].
\end{aligned}
$$

Notice from the previous derivation that

$$
\begin{aligned}
E_t\left[A_T^Q\right] &= \int_{-\infty}^{\infty} \frac{\exp(s)}{\sigma\sqrt{T-t}}\phi\left(\frac{s - (\ln(A_t) + (r - \sigma^2/2)(T-t))}{\sigma\sqrt{T-t}}\right)ds \\
&= \int_{-\infty}^{\infty} \exp\left(\sigma\sqrt{T-t}z + \ln(A_t) + \left(r - \frac{\sigma^2}{2}\right)(T-t)\right)\phi(z)dz \\
&= \exp\left(\ln(A_t) + \left(r - \frac{\sigma^2}{2}\right)(T-t)\right)\exp\left(\frac{\sigma^2}{2}(T-t)\right) \\
&= \exp(r(T-t))A_t.
\end{aligned}
$$

From this observation and the price of equity,

$$
\begin{aligned}
B(A_t, t) &= \exp(-r(T-t))E_t\left[A_T^Q\right] - \exp(-r(T-t))E_t\left[\max\{A_T^Q - M, 0\}\right] \\
&= A_t - A_t\Phi(d_1) + \exp(-r(T-t))M\Phi(d_2) \quad\quad (7.7) \\
&= A_t(1 - \Phi(d_1)) + \exp(-r(T-t))M\Phi(d_2).
\end{aligned}
$$

The value of the levered firm is the sum of the prices of two securities. Then, the levered firm value $V_L(A_t, t)$ is

$$
\begin{aligned}
V_L(A_t, t) &= S(A_t, t) + B(A_t, t) \\
&= A_t.
\end{aligned}
\quad\quad (7.8)
$$

Therefore, the value of the levered firm matches the value of the firm's asset. If the firm is unlevered, its equity holder is the only claim holder of the firm. He just receives the value of the firm's asset A_T at the maturity. He does not receive any dividend until then. Let the price of equity for the unlevered firm be $V_U(A_t, t)$. The terminal value satisfies

$$V_U(A_T, T) = A_T.$$

Because there is no dividend, equation (7.5) suggests that

$$
\begin{aligned}
V_U(A_t, t) &= \exp(-r(T - t))E_t\big[V_U(A_T^Q, T)\big] \\
&= \exp(-r(T - t))E_t\big[A_T^Q\big] \\
&= A_t.
\end{aligned}
\tag{7.9}
$$

Therefore, equations (7.8) and (7.9) suggest that the equity price of the unlevered firm, which is the unlevered firm value, matches the value of the firm's asset.

In summary, I claim the following:

- **Debt and equity prices under Merton (1974):** The prices of debt, equity, and unlevered equity are characterized by equations (7.6), (7.7), and (7.9), respectively. The values of levered and unlevered firms are identical.

This result suggests that capital structure does not affect firm value. Based on realistic parameters, I plot the derived formulas of equity and debt values as well as unlevered equity value. Figure 7.1 presents the values of these securities where $\sigma = 0.25$, $M = 20$, and $r = 0.06$. The top panel shows the value of unlevered equity. Like the payoff of unlevered equity at maturity, the value of unlevered equity is equal to the asset value, regardless of time to maturity. In accordance with this observation, the top panel shows that the value of unlevered equity is represented as a 45-degree line. The bottom panel shows the values of debt and equity for a levered firm. I show both the payoffs of debt and equity at maturity ($T = t$), matching to the payoffs summarized in Table 7.1, and the values of debt and equity before maturity ($T = t + 1$). Unlike the payoffs of debt and equity at maturity, the values of debt and equity are smooth, increasing functions of the asset value. These functions converge to the payoffs of debt and equity at maturity, as the time to maturity becomes shorter.

Intuitively, the value of equity for a levered firm increases in the volatility of the asset value at maturity, conditional on the information currently available, as its terminal value is the convex function of the asset value at maturity. The volatility of the asset value at maturity is larger when there is more time to maturity. Therefore, the bottom panel of Figure 7.1 shows that the equity value is larger when there is more time to maturity.

On the other hand, debt value decreases in the volatility of the asset value at maturity, as its terminal value is the concave function of the asset value at maturity. Consequently, the bottom panel of Figure 7.1 shows that the debt value is smaller when there is more time to maturity.

Figure 7.2 presents the values of debt and equity for various levels of σ while keeping the same parameters except for σ and setting $T = t + 1$. The figure suggests that equity value rises by higher percentage volatility of the asset value process but that debt value decreases in it. This finding is also in line with the earlier hypothesis.

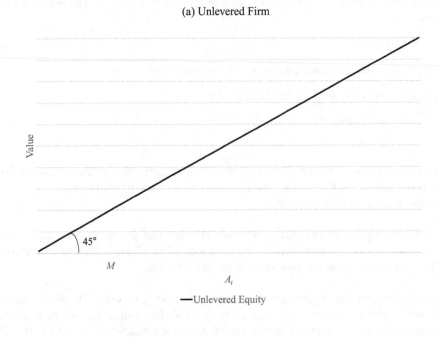

(a) Unlevered Firm

(b) Levered Firm

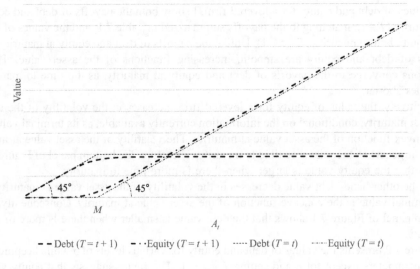

Figure 7.1 Values of Securities

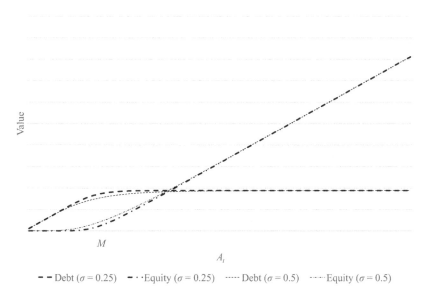

M

A_t

- - Debt ($\sigma = 0.25$)   - · Equity ($\sigma = 0.25$)   ····· Debt ($\sigma = 0.5$)   ······ Equity ($\sigma = 0.5$)

Figure 7.2 Values of Securities by Various Asset Volatilities

The previous observations are also provable through comparative static analysis. Before doing this analysis, I show how d_1 and d_2 are related:

$$-\frac{d_1^2}{2} + \frac{d_2^2}{2} = -\ln(A_t/M) - r(T-t).$$

Then, the partial derivative of equity price with respect to asset value (delta) is

$$
\begin{aligned}
\frac{\partial S(A_t,t)}{\partial A_t} &= \Phi(d_1) + A_t\phi(d_1)\frac{\partial d_1}{\partial A_t} - \exp(-r(T-t))M\phi(d_2)\frac{\partial d_2}{\partial A_t} \\
&= \Phi(d_1) + \frac{1}{\sigma\sqrt{T-t}}\left(\phi(d_1) - \exp(-r(T-t))\frac{M}{A_t}\phi(d_2)\right) \\
&= \Phi(d_1) + \frac{1}{\sigma\sqrt{T-t}}(\phi(d_1) - \exp(-\ln(A_t/M) - r(T-t))\phi(d_2)) \\
&= \Phi(d_1) \\
&\quad + \frac{1}{\sigma\sqrt{2\pi}\sqrt{T-t}}\left(\exp(-d_1^2/2) - \exp(-\ln(A_t/M) - r(T-t))\exp(-d_2^2/2)\right) \\
&= \Phi(d_1) + \frac{1}{\sigma\sqrt{2\pi}\sqrt{T-t}}\left(\exp(-d_1^2/2) - \exp(-d_1^2/2)\right) \\
&= \Phi(d_1) \geq 0.
\end{aligned}
$$

$$(7.10)$$

Also, the partial derivative of equity price with respect to time to maturity (theta) is

$$\frac{\partial S(A_t, t)}{\partial (T-t)} = A_t \phi(d_1) \frac{\partial d_1}{\partial (T-t)} - \exp(-r(T-t)) M \phi(d_2) \frac{\partial d_2}{\partial (T-t)}$$
$$+ r \exp(-r(T-t)) M \Phi(d_2)$$

$$= A_t \left(\phi(d_1) \frac{\partial d_1}{\partial (T-t)} - \underbrace{\exp(-\ln(A_t/M) - r(T-t)) \phi(d_2)}_{\phi(d_1)} \frac{\partial d_2}{\partial (T-t)} \right)$$
$$+ r \exp(-r(T-t)) M \Phi(d_2)$$

$$= A_t \phi(d_1) \left(\frac{\partial d_1}{\partial (T-t)} - \frac{\partial d_2}{\partial (T-t)} \right) + r \exp(-r(T-t)) M \Phi(d_2)$$

$$= A_t \phi(d_1) \frac{\sigma}{2\sqrt{T-t}} + r \exp(-r(T-t)) M \Phi(d_2) \geq 0.$$

$$(7.11)$$

Finally, the partial derivative of equity price with respect to percentage volatility (vega) is

$$\frac{\partial S(A_t, t)}{\partial \sigma} = A_t \phi(d_1) \frac{\partial d_1}{\partial \sigma} - \exp(-r(T-t)) M \phi(d_2) \frac{\partial d_2}{\partial \sigma}$$

$$= A_t \left(\phi(d_1) \frac{\partial d_1}{\partial \sigma} - \underbrace{\exp(-\ln(A_t/M) - r(T-t)) \phi(d_2)}_{\phi(d_1)} \frac{\partial d_2}{\partial \sigma} \right) \qquad (7.12)$$

$$= A_t \phi(d_1) \left(\frac{\partial d_1}{\partial \sigma} - \frac{\partial d_2}{\partial \sigma} \right)$$

$$= A_t \phi(d_1) \sqrt{T-t} \geq 0.$$

Because $B(A_t, t) = A_t - S(A_t, t)$, $\partial B(A_t, t)/\partial A_t = 1 - \partial S(A_t, t)/\partial A_t \geq 0$, $\partial B(A_t, t)/\partial (T-t) = -\partial S(A_t, t)/\partial (T-t) \leq 0$, and $\partial B(A_t, t)/\partial \sigma = -\partial S(A_t, t)/\partial \sigma \leq 0$.

Thus, I claim the following:

- **Comparative statics of debt and equity prices:** The delta, theta, and vega of equity price are characterized by equations (7.10) through (7.12), respectively. Correspondingly, those of debt price are $1 - \partial S(A_t, t)/\partial A_t$, $-\partial S(A_t, t)/\partial (T-t)$, and $-\partial S(A_t, t)/\partial \sigma$, respectively. Equity and debt prices increase in the asset value. The equity price also increases in the time to maturity and the percentage volatility of the asset value process. On the other hand, the debt price decreases in the time to maturity and the percentage volatility of the asset value process.

7.4 Derivative valuation under a stationary case

One difficulty in acquiring an analytically attractive pricing formula is that equation (7.2) is a partial differential equation (PDE). Unless the payoff structure is extremely simple as in European options, closed-form solutions are hard to attain. However, when securities are stationary in the sense that security holders face the same situation every time, given the value of an underlying asset, the prices of these securities do not depend on time t. In this case, the first term in equation (7.2) is zero. Then, equation (7.2) becomes the second-order linear differential equation as follows:

$$\frac{\partial f_k}{\partial A_t} r A_t + \frac{1}{2} \frac{\partial^2 f_k}{\partial A_t^2} \sigma^2 A_t^2 - r f_k + c_k \ = \ 0. \tag{7.13}$$

For the rest of this section, I consider the special case where c_k is constant. The solution of this ordinary differential equation (ODE) starts from finding its trivial solution that does not depend on A_t. I can immediately find that such a solution is $f_k = c_k/r$. Consider a solution of its *homogeneous* version:

$$\frac{\partial f_k}{\partial A_t} r A_t + \frac{1}{2} \frac{\partial^2 f_k}{\partial A_t^2} \sigma^2 A_t^2 - r f_k \ = \ 0.$$

Let g_k be a solution to the homogeneous equation. Then, $f_k = g_k + c_k/r$ is the solution of equation (7.13). This implies that if g_k is attained, the solution of equation (7.13) is also attainable. Suppose $g_k = A_t^x$. Then,

$$\frac{\partial g_k}{\partial A_t} r A_t + \frac{1}{2} \frac{\partial^2 g_k}{\partial A_t^2} \sigma^2 A_t^2 - r g_k \ = \ 0$$

$$\Updownarrow$$

$$\frac{1}{2} \sigma^2 x(x-1) + rx - r \ = \ 0.$$

The two roots for the preceding equation are $x = 1, -2r/\sigma^2$. Then, $g_k = A_t, A_t^{-2r/\sigma^2}$ are two separate solutions to the homogeneous equation. Trivially, any linear combination of the two solutions also becomes the solution of the homogeneous equation. Then, setting $g_k = a_1 A_t + a_2 A_t^{-2r/\sigma^2}$, where a_1 and a_2 are arbitrary constants, I find the solution of equation (7.13) is as follows:

$$f_k \ = \ \frac{c_k}{r} + a_1 A_t + a_2 A_t^{-2r/\sigma^2}. \tag{7.14}$$

The remaining question is whether the solution other than the previous form exists. In fact, it is proved in mathematics that there are no other forms of the solution of equation (7.13). I omit the proof as it is not essential for the readers of corporate finance.

Then, I claim the following:

• **Solution for derivative pricing equation under a stationary case:** The solution to the second-order linear differential equation (7.13) is equation (7.14).

There are two indeterminate constants in the solution. To fix them, I need two *boundary conditions* that regulate the shape of the solution so that it attains a certain required value under a specified condition.

7.5 Trade-off theory revisited

Leland (1994) uses the derivative valuation method under a stationary case to solve the optimal capital structure of a firm. His model is based on the trade-off theory I covered in Chapter 3. It considers each component of a firm's value, such as debt value, the tax benefit of debt, and bankruptcy costs, as the derivative of a firm's asset value. Then, the evaluation of each component becomes easier, as it is the solution of the second-order linear differential equation. Also, it becomes more realistic than its correspondence in the classic trade-off theory, because it moves over time as a firm's asset value follows a stochastic process.

In his model, the firm issues a perpetual bond with a coupon C. Unlike a bond with a finite maturity, a perpetual bond is stationary in the sense that it only depends on a firm's current asset value A_t and does not depend on t. I hence denote the bond value by $B(A_t)$ as a function of A_t. When A_t drops below A_B, a firm's ownership is transferred to bondholders. kA_B is default cost, so bond holders receive $(1 - k)A_B$ at default $(0 < k < 1)$. Again, default condition only depends on the level of a firm's asset value, not t. Then, the value of bankruptcy costs is also stationary and is denoted as a function of A_t by $BC(A_t)$. Finally, I assume a corporate tax rate is τ $(0 < \tau < 1)$. The coupon expense is tax-deductible, so the stream of a tax benefit of debt is τC. When the firm defaults, there is no tax benefit. Because the maturity of a bond is infinite and the default threshold does not depend on t, the tax benefit of debt is also a function of A_t. I denote the tax benefit of debt as a function of A_t by $TB(A_t)$. In summary, each component can be characterized by equation (7.13), with the coupon described in the first column of Table 7.2.

Let us start by evaluating the bond of the firm. Replacing f_k by B and c_k by C and using formula (7.15), the bond's value at $A_t \geq A_B$ is

$$B(A_t) = \frac{C}{r} + a_1 A_t + a_2 A_t^{-2r/\sigma^2}.$$

As $A_t \to \infty$, the bond becomes default-free. In this case, the value of the bond is the value of a safe bond with a coupon C, which is equal to C/r. Moreover, as $A_t \to A_B$, the bond value becomes $(1-k)A_B$. The two boundary conditions are therefore $\lim_{A_t \to \infty} B(A_t) = C/r$ and $\lim_{A_t \to A_B} B(A_t) = (1 - k)A_B$. From the first boundary condition, $a_1 = 0$. With this, from the second boundary condition, I find

$$(1 - k)A_B = \frac{C}{r} + a_2 A_B^{-2r/\sigma^2}$$

$$\Updownarrow$$

$$a_2 = \left((1 - k)A_B - \frac{C}{r} \right) A_B^{2r/\sigma^2}.$$

Table 7.2 Summary of Coupons and Boundary Conditions

f_k	c_k	$A_t \to A_B$	$A_t \to \infty$
B	C	$(1-k)A_B$	C/r
BC	0	kA_B	0
TB	τC	0	$\tau C/r$

Thus,

$$
\begin{aligned}
B(A_t) &= \frac{C}{r} + \left((1-k)A_B - \frac{C}{r} \right) A_B^{2r/\sigma^2} A_t^{-2r/\sigma^2} \\
&= \frac{C}{r}(1 - (A_t/A_B)^{-2r/\sigma^2}) + (1-k)A_B(A_t/A_B)^{-2r/\sigma^2}.
\end{aligned}
\tag{7.15}
$$

In this way, the bond value is characterized as the weighted average of the default-free bond value (C/r) and the bond value at default $((1-k)A_B)$. The weight is $1 - (A_t/A_B)^{-2r/\sigma^2}$ and $(A_t/A_B)^{-2r/\sigma^2}$, where $(A_t/A_B)^{-2r/\sigma^2}$ is almost like the risk-neutral probability of reaching A_B from A_t. More precisely, the weight is the value of the zero-coupon security that attains 1 at A_B and converges to 0 as $A_t \to \infty$. Indeed, the price of such a security based on formula (7.14) with the two boundary conditions is $a_1 A_t + a_2 A_t^{-2r/\sigma^2}$, where $a_1 = 0$ and $a_2 A_B^{-2r/\sigma^2} = 1$, which is equal to $(A_t/A_B)^{-2r/\sigma^2}$. Thus, the bond value is the average of default-free value and the value at default weighted by the probability of survival and default.

Next, I evaluate the firm's bankruptcy costs. In another interpretation, it is the default insurance that covers bankruptcy costs at default. Replacing f_k by BC and c_k by 0 and using formula (7.15), the value of the insurance at $A_t \geq A_B$ is

$$
BC(A_t) = a_1 A_t + a_2 A_t^{-2r/\sigma^2}.
$$

As $A_t \to \infty$, the value of the insurance becomes 0 as there is almost no chance of default. Moreover, as $A_t \to A_B$, the value of the insurance becomes kA_B. The two boundary conditions are therefore $\lim_{A_t \to \infty} BC(A_t) = 0$ and $\lim_{A_t \to A_B} BC(A_t) = kA_B$. From the first boundary condition, $a_1 = 0$. With this, from the second boundary condition, I find

$$
kA_B = a_2 A_B^{-2r/\sigma^2}
$$

$$
\Updownarrow
$$

$$
a_2 = kA_B A_B^{2r/\sigma^2}.
$$

Thus,

$$
\begin{aligned}
BC(A_t) &= kA_B A_B^{2r/\sigma^2} A_t^{-2r/\sigma^2} \\
&= kA_B(A_t/A_B)^{-2r/\sigma^2}.
\end{aligned}
\tag{7.16}
$$

In this way, the value of bankruptcy costs is characterized as the payoff at default multiplied by the term representing default probability $(A_t/A_B)^{-2r/\sigma^2}$, which is the value of the zero-coupon security that attains 1 at A_B and converges to 0 as $A_t \to \infty$.

Last, I evaluate the firm's tax benefit of debt. Replacing f_k by TB and c_k by τC and using formula (7.14), the value at $A_t \geq A_B$ is

$$
TB(A_t) = \frac{\tau C}{r} + a_1 A_t + a_2 A_t^{-2r/\sigma^2}.
$$

As $A_t \to \infty$, the value of the firm's tax benefit of debt becomes $\tau C/r$ as there is almost no chance of default. Moreover, as $A_t \to A_B$, the value of the tax benefit becomes 0. The two boundary conditions are therefore $\lim_{A_t \to \infty} TB(A_t) = \tau C/r$ and $\lim_{A_t \to A_B} TB(A_t) = 0$. From the first boundary condition, $a_1 = 0$. With this, from the second boundary condition, I find

$$0 = \frac{\tau C}{r} + a_2 A_B^{-2r/\sigma^2}$$

$$\Updownarrow$$

$$a_2 = -\frac{\tau C}{r} A_B^{2r/\sigma^2}.$$

Thus,

$$
\begin{aligned}
TB(A_t) &= \frac{\tau C}{r} - \frac{\tau C}{r} A_B^{2r/\sigma^2} A_t^{-2r/\sigma^2} \\
&= \frac{\tau C}{r} \left(1 - (A_t/A_B)^{-2r/\sigma^2}\right).
\end{aligned}
\tag{7.17}
$$

In this way, the value of the tax benefit is characterized as the default-free value of the tax benefit multiplied by the term representing survival probability, $1 - (A_t/A_B)^{-2r/\sigma^2}$.

In summary, the boundary conditions described in the second and third columns of Table 7.2 determine the values of the preceding securities.

Firm value is a firm's asset value plus the tax benefit of debt minus bankruptcy costs, so the firm's value $V(A_t)$ is

$$V(A_t) = A_t + TB(A_t) - BC(A_t).
\tag{7.18}$$

Also, the value of a firm's equity is firm value minus the value of debt. Thus, a firm's equity value $E(A_t)$ is

$$E(A_t) = V(A_t) - B(A_t).
\tag{7.19}$$

Leland (1994) considers equity holders determine A_B *ex post* after raising funds from bondholders. This is because equity holders cannot credibly promise their default decisions to bondholders. Although they try to promise the *ex ante* optimal level of default threshold that increases the amount paid in by bondholders more than reduces the value of equity, they have incentives to deviate from their promise *ex post* after receiving the funds from bondholders as it raises their equity value *ex post*. Then, the optimal threshold A_B^* maximizes the value of equity instead of the firm's value:

$$A_B^* = \arg \max_{A_B} E(A_t).$$

Setting $X = 2r/\sigma^2$, the first-order condition requires

$$(X+1)kA_B^{*X}A_t^{-X} + X\frac{\tau C}{r}A_B^{*X-1}A_t^{-X} = \frac{C}{r}XA_B^{*X-1}A_t^{-X} - (1-k)(X+1)A_B^{*X}A_t^{-X}$$

$$\updownarrow$$

$$(X+1)A_B^* + X\frac{\tau C}{r} = \frac{C}{r}X \tag{7.20}$$

$$\updownarrow$$

$$A_B^* = (1-\tau)\frac{C}{r}\frac{X}{1+X}.$$

Finally, Leland (1994) considers that equity holders determine C ex ante before raising funds from bondholders. Unlike the default threshold, equity holders are asssumed to be able to promise the payment of a constant coupon. Plausibly, this is because such a coupon payment can be made automatically via a blockchain technology, for example. Therefore, equity holders try to maximize the joint surplus of equity value and the amount paid in by bondholders (debt value). Then, the optimal threshold C^* maximizes the firm's value at the initial period ($t = 0$) as follows:

$$C^* = \arg\max_C V(A_0) \text{ s.t. } A_B = A_B^*.$$

At $A_B = A_B^*$, firm value becomes

$$A_t + \frac{\tau C}{r}\left(1 - \left(\frac{A_t}{A_B^*}\right)^{-X}\right)$$

$$-kA_B^*\left(\frac{A_t}{A_B^*}\right)^{-X} = A_t + \frac{\tau C}{r}\left(1 - \left(\frac{A_t}{A_B^*}\right)^{-X} - \frac{rkA_B^{*X+1}}{\tau C}A_t^{-X}\right)$$

$$= A_t + \frac{\tau C}{r}\left(1 - \left(A_B^{*X} + \frac{rkA_B^{*X+1}}{\tau C}\right)A_t^{-X}\right)$$

$$= A_t + \frac{\tau C}{r}\left(1 - \left(1 + \frac{rkA_B^*}{\tau C}\right)A_B^{*X}A_t^{-X}\right)$$

$$= A_t + \frac{\tau C}{r}\times$$

$$\left(1 - \left(1 + \frac{k(1-\tau)}{\tau}\frac{X}{1+X}\right)\left(\frac{1-\tau}{r}\frac{X}{1+X}\right)^X\left(\frac{A_t}{C}\right)^{-X}\right)$$

$$= A_t + \frac{\tau C}{r}\left(1 - h\left(\frac{A_t}{C}\right)^{-X}\right),$$

where $h = (1 + X + kX(1 - \tau)/\tau)m$ and $m = ((1 - \tau)X/r(1 + X))^X/(1 + X)$. Then, the first-order condition requires

$$\frac{\tau}{r}\left(1 - h\left(\frac{A_0}{C^*}\right)^{-X}\right) = \frac{\tau C^*}{r}hX\left(\frac{A_0}{C^*}\right)^{-X-1}A_0/C^{*2}$$

$$\updownarrow$$

$$\left(\frac{A_0}{C^*}\right)^{X} - h = hX$$

$$\updownarrow$$ (7.21)

$$\left(\frac{A_0}{C^*}\right)^{X} = h(1 + X)$$

$$\updownarrow$$

$$C^* = A_0(h(1 + X))^{-1/X}.$$

Then, the default threshold A_B^* evaluated at the optimal coupon C^* becomes

$$A_B^* = (1 - \tau)\frac{A_0(h(1 + X))^{-1/X}}{r}\frac{X}{1 + X}$$

$$= A_0(m/h)^{1/X}.$$ (7.22)

Correspondingly, the initial firm value is

$$V^*(A_0) = A_0 + \frac{\tau A_0(h(1 + X))^{-1/X}}{r}\left(1 - h\left(\frac{A_0}{A_0(h(1 + X))^{-1/X}}\right)^{-X}\right)$$

$$= A_0\left(1 + \frac{\tau}{r}(h(1 + X))^{-1/X}\frac{X}{1 + X}\right).$$ (7.23)

The initial debt value is

$$B^*(A_0) = \frac{C^*}{r}\left(1 - \left(\frac{A_0}{(1 - \tau)C^*X/r(1 + X)}\right)^{-X}\right)$$

$$+ (1 - k)(1 - \tau)\frac{C^*}{r}\frac{X}{1 + X}\left(\frac{A_0}{(1 - \tau)C^*X/r(1 + X)}\right)^{-X}$$

$$= \frac{C^*}{r}\left(1 - \left(\frac{A_0}{(1 - \tau)C^*X/r(1 + X)}\right)^{-X}\right)$$

$$+ \frac{C^*}{r}\frac{(1 - k)(1 - \tau)X}{1 + X}\left(\frac{A_0}{(1 - \tau)C^*X/r(1 + X)}\right)^{-X}$$

$$= \frac{C^*}{r}\left(1 - \left(\frac{(1 - \tau)X}{r(1 + X)}\right)^{X}\left(\frac{C^*}{A_0}\right)^{X} + \frac{(1 - k)(1 - \tau)X}{1 + X}\left(\frac{(1 - \tau)X}{r(1 + X)}\right)^{X}\left(\frac{C^*}{A_0}\right)^{X}\right)$$

$$= \frac{C^*}{r}\left(1 - (1 + X - (1 - k)(1 - \tau)X)m\left(\frac{C^*}{A_0}\right)^X\right)$$

$$= \frac{C^*}{r}\left(1 - q\left(\frac{C^*}{A_0}\right)^X\right)$$

$$= A_0(h(1 + X))^{-1/X}\left(1 - q\left(\frac{A_0(h(1 + X))^{-1/X}}{A_0}\right)^X\right)/r \qquad (7.24)$$

$$= A_0(h(1 + X))^{-1/X}\left(1 - \frac{q}{h(1 + X)}\right)/r,$$

where $q = (1 + X - (1 - k)(1 - \tau)X)m$. This completes the characterization of the optimal capital structure.

In summary, I claim the following:

- **Optimal capital structure under Leland (1994):** The optimal capital structure is characterized by equations (7.21) through (7.24). Specifically, the optimal leverage is $B^*(A_0)/V^*(A_0)$, where $B^*(A_0)$ and $V^*(A_0)$ are defined by equations (7.24) and (7.23), respectively. Moreover, equity value is $V^*(A_0) - B^*(A_0)$.

Then, I am able to predict the relationship between the optimal capital structure of a firm and the primitive parameters.

I start by considering how the initial asset value A_0 affects the optimal capital structure. Equations (7.21) through (7.24) suggest that the optimal coupon and default threshold, as well as firm and debt values (and hence equity values), are homogeneous of degree 1; each is proportional to A_0. This implies that the optimal leverage $B^*(A_0)/V^*(A_0)$ is invariant to the initial asset value A_0.

Based on realistic parameters, I compute the values of equity and debt as well as the firm's value. In particular, I choose parameters in accordance with Leland (1998), where $k = 0.25$, $\tau = 0.2$, $\sigma = 0.25$, $r = 0.06$, $A_0 = 100$. I find debt value is 73 while the equity value is 38. The firm's value is 111. Consequently, the optimal leverage is 66%.

I next investigate whether Leland's model is consistent with the comparative statics of the trade-off theory I derive in Chapter 3. Table 7.3 presents how security values vary by local perturbation of each parameter while keeping the other parameters set to those previously stated. In the top panel, I move the bankruptcy costs k. As k changes from 0.2 to 0.3, the debt value decreases while the equity value increases, so that the leverage decreases from 68% to 64%. In the middle panel, I move the corporate tax rate τ from 0.15 to 0.25. As τ rises, the debt value increases while the equity value decreases so that the leverage increases from 61% to 70%. Hence, the optimal leverage and debt value decrease in bankruptcy costs k and increase in corporate tax rate τ, which is consistent with the prediction of the trade-off theory (see Chapter 3).

In the bottom panel, I move the percentage volatility σ from 0.2 to 0.3. As σ rises, the debt value decreases while the equity value increases so that the leverage decreases from 71% to 62%. It therefore shows the negative effect of the volatility of the asset value process on the debt value and the optimal leverage. This finding is consistent with the result of comparative statics discussed in the section of Merton's model.

Table 7.3 Summary of Simulation Outcomes

Parameter	Debt	Equity	Leverage
k			
0.2	76	36	68%
0.25	73	38	66%
0.3	71	40	64%
τ			
0.15	65	42	61%
0.2	73	38	66%
0.25	81	35	70%
σ			
0.2	80	33	71%
0.25	73	38	66%
0.3	68	42	62%

7.6 Discussion

Although Merton's and Leland's models consider far more realistic situations than traditional frameworks, their derived formulas of equity and debt are surprisingly simple. After their success, the following work has been improving their work by adding new features.

One issue with Leland (1994) is that equation (7.20) suggests that a firm's default threshold decreases in the corporate tax rate. Intuitively, a firm's net income would decrease in the corporate tax rate, and hence, its default threshold would go up. The gap between this intuition and the preceding result arises from the fact that Leland (1994) derives the value of equity *not based on a firm's net income*. We, however, note that Leland (1994) resolves this problem by endogenizing a firm's coupon level. Indeed, equation (7.22) suggests that a firm's default threshold increases in the corporate tax rate, which is consistent with our conjecture. To address this issue more fundamentally, Goldstein et al. (2001; GJL henceforth) develop a "flow-based" model of capital structure. In their model, an underlying asset value process A_t is replaced by the process of earnings before interest and taxes (EBIT).

Another problem of Leland (1994) is that it predicts an unrealistically high level of leverage under reasonable parameters. The caveat is that it still predicts a reasonable level of leverage when the default threshold is exogenous. GJL resolves this issue by allowing firms to lever up when EBIT goes up. With this change, GIJ predict a reasonable level of leverage under an endogenous default threshold choice.

GJL's (2001) paper, as well as Leland (1994) and Merton (1974), however, assume investment policy is exogenous. To overcome this issue, Leland (1998) integrates the investment decisions with the financing decisions in which a firm may increase the volatility of its asset value after debt is issued. He then shows a firm's risk-shifting incentive and quantifies the agency cost of overinvestment. In this respect, Leland (1998) is considered an updated framework of the agency theory that I covered in Chapter 4.

For further extensions of these models, I recommend interested readers see the review by Sundaresan (2013).

Bibliography

Goldstein, R., Ju, N., and Leland, H. (2001). An EBIT-based model of dynamic capital structure. *Journal of Business*, 74(4):483–512.

Leland, H. (1994). Corporate debt value, bond covenants, and optimal capital structure. *Journal of Finance*, 49(4):1213–52.

Leland, H. (1998). Agency costs, risk management, and capital structure. *Journal of Finance*, 53 (4):1213–43.

Merton, R. (1974). On the pricing of corporate debt: The risk structure of interest rates. *Journal of Finance*, 29(2):449–70.

Sundaresan, S. (2013). A review of Merton's model of the firm's capital structure with its wide applications. *Annual Review of Financial Economics*, 5(1):21–41.

8

CAPITAL STRUCTURE OF A BANK

8.1 Two roles of a bank

Why does a bank exist? One significant friction in our economy is unpredictable preference shocks that affect households' consumption schedules. In order for households to smooth their consumption, they need to hold liquid securities that are withdrawable at any time they want. In order for an economy to provide such securities, there has to be an institution that aggregates households' preference shocks to wash away shocks at the economy level. Bryant (1980) suggests that a bank fulfills that role by issuing demand deposits to its creditors. Another friction is the difficulty of monitoring entrepreneurs. When households try to invest in entrepreneurs, each of them may not have enough skill and time in monitoring entrepreneurs. More severely, even if each has enough skill and time for monitoring them, each may not be willing to monitor them, anticipating some other households will monitor them. In other words, a free-rider problem occurs. Under either circumstance, entrepreneurs deviate from maximizing a firm's value to pursue their own interests. To avoid this problem, a bank aggregates information and skill for monitoring entrepreneurs on behalf of dispersed households (Diamond, 1984).

In summary, there are two roles of a bank: *liquidity provision* and *delegated monitoring*. For the rest of this chapter, we see (1) how to implement liquidity provision, (2) how this role aggravates a bank's delegated monitoring role, and (3) how to fix this dilemma by modulating a firm's capital structure.

8.2 Bank run and deposit insurance

Diamond and Dybvig (1983) wrote a pioneering paper on how a bank's role of liquidity provision affects its capital structure and makes it vulnerable to liquidity shortage. The paper ultimately proposes deposit insurance as a policy to eliminate this fragility.

They consider a three-period model. At $t = 0$, consumers receive 1 unit of a good and make investment decisions. The good can be freely stored from $t = x$ to $t = x + 1$ ($x = 0, 1$). Also, it can be invested through an *illiquid* technology that will pay R per a unit of invested goods at $t = 2$ ($R > 1$) if the investment is not liquidated at $t = 1$, and 1 at $t = 1$ if the investment is liquidated at $t = 1$. This suggests that consumers have no incentives to store goods from $t = 0$ to $t = 1$. Therefore, without loss of generality, I assume all consumers invest in the illiquid technology at $t = 0$.

There are two types of consumers: Type 1 and Type 2. Type 1 consumers have a utility function $u(C_1^1, C_2^1) = u(C_1^1)$, where C_j^i denotes the consumption at $t = j$ by Type i. On the other hand, Type 2 consumers have a utility function $u(C_1^2, C_2^2) = \rho u(C_2^2)$, where $R^{-1} < \rho \le 1$. Consumers do not know their types at $t = 0$ and notice their types at $t = 1$. In this way, the model captures consumers' unpredictable preference shocks. I denote the probability of becoming Type 1 by π_1 ($0 < \pi_1 < 1$). The total population of consumers is 1.

I start by characterizing equilibrium with trade without a bank. In particular, at $t = 1$, a security that will pay 1 unit of a good at $t = 2$ is available. Who buys the security at $t = 1$? Type 1 consumers know that they gain from current consumption but not from future ones. On the other hand, Type 2 consumers know that they gain from future consumption but not from current ones. Therefore, a Type 2 consumer buys the security from a Type 1 consumer. Let p be the price of the security.

If $p < R^{-1}$, Type 1 consumers are better off when they liquidate their investment, so they have no incentives to sell the securities. To see why, suppose Type 1 consumers issue ϵ units of the securities ($\epsilon > 0$) and raise $p\epsilon$ at $t = 1$. They will pay ϵ at $t = 2$ and so do not liquidate $R^{-1}\epsilon$ of their investment at $t = 1$. Then, they liquidate $1 - R^{-1}\epsilon$ of their investment and consume $1 - R^{-1}\epsilon + p\epsilon = 1 - (R^{-1} - p)\epsilon < 1$ at $t = 1$. Thus, they are strictly better off if they fully liquidate their investment at $t = 1$, because they can consume 1 unit of a good at $t = 1$ by doing so.

If $p > R^{-1}$, Type 2 consumers are better off when they do not liquidate their investment at all, so they have no incentives to buy the securities. To see why, suppose Type 2 consumers buy ϵ units of the securities and pay $p\epsilon$ at $t = 1$. They liquidate $p\epsilon$ at $t = 1$, so their investment will pay $R(1 - p\epsilon)$ at $t = 2$. Then, they will consume $R(1 - p\epsilon) + \epsilon = R - (Rp - 1)\epsilon < R$ at $t = 2$. Thus, they are strictly better off if they keep their investment unliquidated at $t = 1$, because they will be able to consume R units of good at $t = 2$ by doing so.

Thus, the only admissible equilibrium security price is $p = R^{-1}$. At this price, both consumers are indifferent between trading and nontrading. Consequently, at an equilibrium with trade, $C_1^1 = 1 - (R^{-1} - p)\epsilon = 1$, $C_2^2 = R - (Rp - 1)\epsilon = R$, where ϵ is an arbitrary trading volume.

I next investigate a social planner's problem. The planner maximizes social surplus at $t = 0$, being subject to the aggregate resource constraint. Let the fraction of investment liquidated at $t = 1$ be s. Considering a planner has no incentives to allocate goods to Type 2 consumers at $t = 1$ and to Type 1 consumers at $t = 2$, his effective constraint is

$$\pi_1 C_1^1 \le s,$$
$$(1 - \pi_1)C_2^2 \le R(1 - s),$$

for *some* s. Then, it is equivalent to

$$\pi_1 C_1^1 + (1 - \pi_1)C_2^2/R \quad \le \quad 1. \tag{8.1}$$

Thus, the planner's problem is

$$\max_{C_1^1, C_2^2} \pi_1 u(C_1^1) + (1 - \pi_1)\rho u(C_2^2) \quad \text{s.t.} \quad (8.1).$$

Assuming $u(.)$ is strictly increasing, the resource constraint binds. Assuming also that $u(.)$ is a strictly concave function (a consumer's risk aversion), the efficient allocation of each agent's consumption satisfies the following first-order condition:

$$\pi_1 u'(C_1^1) - (1 - \pi_1)\rho R u'(R(1 - \pi_1 C_1^1)/(1 - \pi_1))\pi_1/(1 - \pi_1) = 0,$$

$$\updownarrow \qquad (8.2)$$

$$u'(C_1^1) - \rho R u'(R(1 - \pi_1 C_1^1)/(1 - \pi_1)) = 0.$$

Defining C_1^1 and $R(1 - \pi_1 C_1^1)/(1 - \pi_1)$, satisfying equation (8.2) as $C_1^*(\pi_1)$ and $C_2^*(\pi_1)$, I claim $C_1^*(\pi_1) > 1, C_2^*(\pi_1) < R, C_2^*(\pi_1) > C_1^*(\pi_1)$, if $-xu''(x)/u'(x) > 1$; that is, relative risk aversion (RRA) exceeds 1. This result comes from the following relationship:

$$\rho R u'(R) \leq R u'(R)$$

$$= \int_1^R \frac{\partial(xu'(x))}{\partial x} dx + u'(1)$$

$$= \int_1^R (u'(x) + xu''(x))dx + u'(1)$$

$$< u'(1),$$

as RRA exceeds 1. If $C_2^*(\pi_1) \geq R$, the preceding relationship suggests that:

$$\rho R u'(C_2^*(\pi_1)) \leq \rho R u'(R)$$

$$< u'(1),$$

because $u''(.) < 0$. Under condition (8.2),

$$u'(C_1^*(\pi_1)) = \rho R u'(C_2^*(\pi_1))$$

$$< u'(1),$$

so $C_1^*(\pi_1) > 1$. However, it violates the resource constraint that requires $C_1^*(\pi_1) \leq 1$ under $C_2^*(\pi_1) \geq R$. Thus, $C_2^*(\pi_1) < R$ is necessary. Hence, $C_1^*(\pi_1) > 1$. Notice that $u'(C_1^*(\pi_1)) > u'(C_2^*(\pi_1))$ under condition (8.2) as $\rho R > 1$, suggesting that $C_2^*(\pi_1) > C_1^*(\pi_1)$.

In summary, I find the consumption of each type under equilibrium with trade and the efficient consumption schedule is as follows:

- **Equilibrium with trade and efficient outcome:** The consumption of each type under a different scenario is described in Table 8.1.

Table 8.1 Summary of Consumption

Scenario	Type 1		Type 2
Equilibrium with trade	1	<	R
	$\wedge$		$\vee$
Efficient outcome	$C_1^*(\pi_1)$	<	$C_2^*(\pi_1)$

This result suggests that the efficient consumption schedule is less polarized than the one at equilibrium with trade. In one interpretation, the planner's objective function is the utility of a consumer expected at $t = 0$. If the RRA is greater than 1, she is risk-averse enough to gain from a smoother consumption schedule than the one at equilibrium with trade.

Finally, I analyze an equilibrium with a bank. For this purpose, I assume the bank exclusively invests in an illiquid technology, perhaps due to superior monitoring skills, on behalf of consumers. The bank issues demand deposits to consumers at $t = 0$. Demand deposits are withdrawable both at $t = 1$ and $t = 2$. When demand deposits are withdrawn, the bank fully or partially liquidates the illiquid technology to pay predetermined coupons. Consumers can invest in demand deposits instead of the illiquid technology at $t = 0$ and still retain the technology of storing wealth from $t = 1$ to $t = 2$. Here, following Diamond and Dybvig (1983), I assume *all consumers purchase demand deposits* at $t = 0$. To justify this assumption, I assume storing wealth from $t = 0$ to $t = 1$ is impossible for consumers. Moreover, I assume no new entry condition. Under this condition, the bank earns zero profit.

I consider a demand deposit pays coupon r_1 per a withdrawer, as long as the bank has assets to be liquidated, at $t = 1$. If the bank has no more assets at $t = 1$, the bank defaults while consumers serviced after default will receive zero. Let f_j be the number of drawers serviced before withdrawer j as a fraction of total consumers. Let f be the total number of consumers who already withdrew at $t = 1$. Specifically, the payoff from a demand deposit at $t = 1$, $v_1(f_j, r_1)$, and $t = 2$, $v_2(f, r_1)$, satisfies

$$
\begin{aligned}
v_1(f_j, r_1) &= \begin{cases} r_1 & \text{if a bank survives } (f_j r_1 < 1), \\ 0 & \text{if a bank defaults } (f_j r_1 \geq 1), \end{cases} \\
v_2(f, r_1) &= \begin{cases} R(1 - r_1 f)/(1 - f) & \text{if a bank survives } (f r_1 < 1), \\ 0 & \text{if a bank defaults } (f r_1 \geq 1). \end{cases}
\end{aligned}
\tag{8.3}
$$

Under payoff schedule (8.3), the jth withdrawer receives r_1 at $t = 1$ if the bank still has assets to be liquidated ($f_j r_1 < 1$). Otherwise, the withdrawer would receive none at $t = 1$ ($f_j r_1 \geq 1$). At $t = 2$, withdrawers equally share returns from remaining assets if the bank leaves some assets unliquidated ($f r_1 < 1$). If there is no remaining asset, they would receive none ($f r_1 \geq 1$). Under payoff schedule (8.3), the bank does not earn any profit. Payoff schedule (8.3) satisfies resource constraint (8.1).

Our first goal is to check whether I can rationalize the consumption schedule under equilibrium with trade and the efficient consumption schedule as an equilibrium with a bank. Equilibrium with a bank is characterized by a pair $\{r_1, f\}$.

Let us start with equilibrium with trade. Suppose consumers anticipate $\{r_1, f\} = \{1, \pi_1\}$ so that any withdrawer at $t = 1$ receives 1, while any withdrawer at $t = 2$ receives R. All Type 1 consumers withdraw deposits at $t = 1$, as they need to consume at $t = 1$. All Type 2 consumers wait until $t = 2$, because they will receive R by doing so, but they receive only 1 at $t = 1$. Hence, $f = \pi_1$. Then, $C_1^1 = 1$ and $C_2^2 = R$. An equilibrium with trade is rationalizable as an equilibrium with a bank.

Let us next consider the efficient consumption schedule. Suppose consumers anticipate $\{r_1, f\} = \{C_1^*(\pi_1), \pi_1\}$ so that any withdrawer at $t = 1$ receives $C_1^*(\pi_1)$, while any withdrawer at $t = 2$ receives $C_2^*(\pi_1)$. All Type 1 consumers withdraw deposits at $t = 1$, as they need to consume at $t = 1$. All Type 2 consumers wait until $t = 2$, because they will receive $C_2^*(\pi_1)$ by doing so, which is strictly greater than $C_1^*(\pi_1)$. Hence, $f = \pi_1$. Consequently, $C_1^1 = C_1^*(\pi_1)$ and $C_2^2 = C_2^*(\pi_1)$. The efficient consumption schedule is rationalizable as an equilibrium with a bank.

So far, I see the benefit of having a bank, as it rationalizes the efficient consumption schedule as an equilibrium. However, Diamond and Dybvig (1983) are rather famous for their unfavorable result of having a bank—a bank run. Suppose consumers anticipate $\{r_1, f\} = \{x, 1\}$, where $x > 1$, so that jth withdrawer at $t = 1$ receives x if $f_j < 1/x$, but 0 if $f_j \geq 1/x$. Any withdrawer at $t = 2$ receives 0. All Type 1 consumers withdraw deposits at $t = 1$, as they need to consume at $t = 1$. All Type 2 consumers also withdraw at $t = 1$, because they would receive 0 *for sure* at $t = 2$ if they waited. Then, $f = 1$. A bank run happens. Therefore, $C_1^1 = x$ or 0 and $C_1^2 = x$ or 0. Notice that this outcome is *ex ante* worse than an equilibrium with trade. To see why, let us focus on the case where $\rho = 1$. Also, consider a consumer's timing of withdrawal is random at $t = 1$. Under these conditions, her expected utility is $u(0)(1 - 1/x) + u(x)/x < u(1)$, as the expected consumption amount is 1 while she is strictly risk-averse. Her expected utility at an equilibrium with trade is $\pi_1 u(1) + (1 - \pi_1)u(R) > u(1)$, on the other hand. Thus, her expected utility at a bank run is strictly smaller than her expected utility at an equilibrium with trade.

In summary, I claim the following:

- **Equilibrium with a bank:** There are at least three types of equilibria with a bank. Each equilibrium is described in Table 8.2.

This result suggests that the presence of multiple equilibria with a bank. Then, there is room for regulatory intervention. If a regulator is able to induce an efficient outcome uniquely, such a policy is welfare-enhancing.

How can a regulator achieve an efficient outcome and eliminate a bank run? The reason why a bank run occurs is Type 2 consumers withdraw demand deposits at $t = 1$ (Type 1 consumers withdraw deposits at $t = 1$ anyway). If the payoff from a deposit at $t = 2$ is *credibly* larger than that at $t = 1$, they do not withdraw at $t = 1$ and wait until $t = 2$. Diamond and Dybvig (1983) propose the *suspension of convertibility* and *deposit insurance* to achieve this goal, depending on whether π_1 is known to a regulator.

When π_1 is known, the suspension of convertibility helps eliminate a bank run and uniquely induce an efficient outcome. Under this scheme, a regulator limits the number

Table 8.2 Summary of Equilibria

Type	r_1	f	C_1^1	C_1^2
Equivalent to equilibrium with trade	1	π_1	1	R
Efficient outcome	$C_1^*(\pi_1)$	π_1	$C_1^*(\pi_1)$	$C_2^*(\pi_1)$
Bank run	x	1	0 or x	0 or x

Note: x is an arbitrary number greater than 1.

of withdrawals at $t = 1$ *ex ante* for promising a Type 2 depositor a payoff of at least $C_2^*(\pi_1)$ at $t = 2$. Specifically,

$$
v_1(f_j) = \begin{cases} C_1^*(\pi_1) & \text{if } f_j \leq \pi_1, \\ 0 & \text{if } f_j > \pi_1, \end{cases}
$$

$$
v_2(f) = \begin{cases} R(1 - C_1^*(\pi_1)f)/(1-f) & \text{if } f \leq \pi_1, \\ C_2^*(\pi_1) & \text{if } f > \pi_1. \end{cases}
$$

(8.4)

Under payoff schedule (8.4), a withdrawer at $t = 1$ receives optimal consumption $C_1^*(\pi_1)$, depending on whether the number of withdrawers serviced before j exceeds the threshold π_1, not whether the bank has remaining assets to be liquidated. Withdrawers at $t = 2$ equally share returns from remaining assets. Note that a bank earns zero profit under payoff schedule (8.4) and that payoff schedule (8.4) satisfies resource constraint (8.1). In practice, payoff schedule (8.4) is implemented by stopping withdrawal when π_1th withdrawer has finished withdrawing demand deposits at $t = 1$. Because $v_2(f) \geq C_2^*(\pi_1)$ and $v_1(f_j) \leq C_1^*(\pi_1)$, $v_1(f_j) < v_2(f)$. Then, as the regulator aimed, Type 2 depositors wait until $t = 2$. f hence becomes π_1. A consumer of each type achieves the efficient consumption schedule.

When π_1 is unknown, deposit insurance helps eliminate a bank run and uniquely induces an efficient outcome. Even if regulators cannot observe π_1, they can commit contingency on the number of withdrawals at the end of $t = 1$. For example, the government adjusts deposit rates *ex post* by taxing or subsidizing withdrawers. Under this scheme, a regulator commits to pay $C_1^*(f)$ contingent on f at $t = 1$ for promising a Type 2 depositor a payoff of $C_2^*(f)$ at $t = 2$. Specifically,

$$
v_1(f) = C_1^*(f),
$$
$$
v_2(f) = C_2^*(f).
$$

(8.5)

Under payoff schedule (8.5), a withdrawer at $t = 1$ receives $C_1^*(f)$, that is, optimal consumption when f of consumers is Type 1. Withdrawers at $t = 2$ equally share returns from remaining assets, so each receives $C_2^*(f)$. Because $C_2^*(\pi_1) > C_1^*(\pi_1)$ for any π_1 as discussed earlier, $C_2^*(f) > C_1^*(f)$ for any f. Then, Type 2 depositors wait until $t = 2$. Consequently, f becomes π_1. A consumer of each type receives the same amount of goods consumed under an efficient equilibrium. Notice a bank earns zero profit under payoff schedule (8.5) and payoff schedule (8.5) satisfies resource constraint (8.1).

Thus, both policies work as commitment devices to induce an efficient equilibrium. In particular, deposit insurance does not require a regulator to know the fraction of Type 1 consumers, which makes deposit insurance a standard regulatory tool for the banking sector.

8.3 Unintended consequence of deposit insurance

The limitation of Diamond and Dybvig (1983) is that it does not endogenize bank risk-taking. Intuitively, in the presence of deposit insurance, creditors do not demand interest rates that commensurate with expected credit losses. When creditors charge the bank a flat-rate premium, the bank does not internalize the full cost of risk-taking. As a result, the bank engages in excessive risk-taking.

To assess this conjecture, I consider a simple model developed by Gropp and Vesala (2001). In their model, bank risk-taking is measured by $1 - m$, where m is monitoring intensity ($m \in [0, 1]$). With probability $1 - m$, the bank's return from investment is zero; hence, it defaults. With probability m, its return from investment is R ($R > 0$). The bank's monitoring cost is βm^2. The bank is funded by depositors (α) and subordinated debt holders ($1 - \alpha$), where $0 < \alpha < 1$. The government insures depositors' claims at default with the probability γ^D, where $0 < \gamma^D < 1$. Let r be the risk-free rate and $\bar{r} - r$ be the risk premium when the bank defaults for sure ($\bar{r} - r > 0$). Then, the deposit rate r^D satisfies $r^D = r + (1 - m)(1 - \gamma^D)(\bar{r} - r)$, where the risk premium is proportional to the probability of default and the probability of being uninsured. On the other hand, the interest rate of subordinated debt r^B satisfies $r^B = r + (1 - m)(\bar{r} - r)$, where the risk premium is only proportional to the probability of default.

A bank maximizes its expected profit by choosing the optimal monitoring intensity:

$$\max_{m} \ mR - r^D \alpha - r^B (1 - \alpha) - \beta m^2.$$

The first-order condition (FOC) for the interior solution requires

$$\underbrace{R + (\bar{r} - r)[\alpha(1 - \gamma^D) + (1 - \alpha)]}_{\text{return at survival + decreases in financing cost}} = \underbrace{2\beta m}_{\text{increases in monitoring cost}}.$$

This result suggests that the optimal monitoring intensity is set to the level at which the marginal value of monitoring (the left-hand side) is equal to the marginal cost of monitoring (the right-hand side). Also, the previous relationship suggests that, under $R + \bar{r} - r < 2\beta$, the optimal monitoring is interior and unique. Under $R + \bar{r} - r < 2\beta$, the optimal monitoring intensity satisfies

$$m^* = \frac{R + (\bar{r} - r)[\alpha(1 - \gamma^D) + (1 - \alpha)]}{2\beta}. \tag{8.6}$$

I next investigate how the optimal monitoring intensity is associated with each parameter. It is easy to find $\partial m^*/\partial \gamma^D < 0$ and $\partial m^*/\partial \alpha < 0$.

I then claim the following:

- **Insured deposits and moral hazard:** If $R + \bar{r} - r < 2\beta$, the optimal monitoring intensity satisfies equation (8.6). Moreover, $\partial m^*/\partial \gamma^D < 0$, $\partial m^*/\partial \alpha < 0$.

This result suggests that both deposit insurance and finance reduce bank monitoring. To resolve this issue, risk-sensitive deposit insurance premiums, for example, a tax payment contingent on default probability $1 - m$, may work, because it penalizes risk-taking by allowing a bank to fully internalize the cost of risk-taking. In reality, however, risk-sensitive deposit insurance premium is hard to implement (Pennacchi, 2009). First, the government cannot monitor the bank's risk management without resources. Second, even if it is possible, it is politically difficult to raise taxes on banks with high default probability. If this occurs, the government appears as if it is pushing failing banks over a cliff.

The other implication from this result is if a bank is more financed by subordinated debt, such as long-term debt, it has larger incentives to make risk-minimizing efforts even in the presence of deposit insurance. This result motivates capital regulation, because a regulator can reduce bank risk-taking by forcing a bank to be financed by subordinated debt or equity-like instruments.

8.4 Capital regulation

To understand the regulatory benefit of bank capital, I study Hellmann et al. (2000). Their model is dynamic but stationary, assuming each of the competing banks uses the same strategy over time. Each bank maximizes its value by choosing its asset type, the level of interest rate it offers to depositors, and its capital level.

In each period, competing banks play the stage game. Bank i offers interest rate r_i for its deposits. It also raises capital k_i as the percentage of its deposits. The cost of capital is ρ. Deposits are insured, so deposit supply only depends on interest rates offered. The deposit supply function is denoted by $D(r_i, r_{-i})$ where $D_1 > 0$ and $D_2 < 0$, meaning it increases in the bank's own interest rate and decreases in the symmetric competitors' rate.[1] Then, the bank's financing cost is $D(r_i, r_{-i})(r_i + \rho k)$, if it survives, and $D(r_i, r_{-i})\rho k$, if it defaults, as it is not liable for interest payment at default. Using the deposits, the bank invests in either prudent or gambling assets. For a prudent asset, the rate of return is α ($\rho > \alpha > 0$). For a gambling asset, the rate of return is γ with probability θ ($\gamma > \alpha$) and 0 with probability $1 - \theta$ ($0 < \theta < 1$). The bank defaults when the asset return is zero, so the bank defaults with probability $1 - \theta$. Also, $\alpha > \theta\gamma$, suggesting that investing in prudent assets is relatively value-enhancing.

Under the preceding condition with discount factor δ ($0 < \delta < 1$), the bank's value from investing in prudent assets is

$$V_P(r_i, r_{-i}, k_i) = D(r_i, r_{-i})(\alpha(1 + k_i) - \rho k_i - r_i) + \delta V_P(r_i, r_{-i}, k_i)$$
$$= D(r_i, r_{-i})(\alpha(1 + k_i) - \rho k_i - r_i)/(1 - \delta).$$

Also, its value from investing in gambling assets is

$$V_G(r_i, r_{-i}, k_i) = D(r_i, r_{-i})(\theta(\gamma(1 + k_i) - r_i) - \rho k_i) + \delta\theta V_G(r_i, r_{-i}, k_i)$$
$$= D(r_i, r_{-i})(\theta(\gamma(1 + k_i) - r_i) - \rho k_i)/(1 - \delta\theta).$$

The bank invests in prudent assets if $V_P(r_i, r_{-i}, k_i) \geq V_G(r_i, r_{-i}, k_i)$. This condition is equivalent to

$$r_i \leq \hat{r}(k_i), \text{ where } \quad \hat{r}(k_i) = (1 - \delta)\frac{\alpha - \theta\gamma}{1 - \theta}(1 + k_i) + \delta(\alpha(1 + k_i) - \rho k_i). \tag{8.7}$$

This result reflects the merit of not paying interest at default, and hence the incentive for gambling, is larger when interest rate r_i is higher.

I start by investigating a symmetric equilibrium without regulation. If a bank invests in prudent assets, it will solve

$$\max_{r_i, k_i} \quad V_P(r_i, r_{-i}, k_i).$$

From the FOC, the optimal interest rate is characterized as a function of k_i and r_{-i}. I denote this function by $R_P(k_i, r_{-i})$. Then, it satisfies

$$R_P(k_i, r_{-i}) = (\alpha(1 + k_i) - \rho k_i)\frac{\epsilon_P}{\epsilon_P + 1}, \tag{8.8}$$

where ϵ_P is interest rate elasticity of deposit supply, $R_P(k_i, r_{-i})D_1/D$. Let k_P be the optimal level of capital. Because $\partial V_P(r_i, r_{-i}, k_i)/\partial k_i < 0$, $k_P = 0$, $\forall r_{-i}$. As the banking sector becomes perfectly competitive ($\epsilon_P \to \infty$),

$$\hat{r}(k_P) = (1 - \delta)(\alpha - \theta(\gamma - \alpha)/(1 - \theta)) + \delta\alpha < \alpha \leftarrow R_P(k_P, r_{-i}), \forall r_{-i}.$$

Therefore, if the banking sector is sufficiently competitive, the bank prefers to invest in gambling assets at the interest rate and the capital level that maximize the value from investing in prudent assets. Because of this incentive for deviation, prudent investment cannot be an equilibrium strategy. On the other hand, if a bank invests in gambling assets, it will solve

$$\max_{r_i, k_i} V_G(r_i, r_{-i}, k_i).$$

From the FOC, the optimal interest rate is characterized as a function of k_i and r_{-i}:

$$R_G(k_i, r_{-i}) = (\gamma(1 + k_i) - \rho k_i/\theta)\frac{\epsilon_G}{\epsilon_G + 1}, \tag{8.9}$$

where ϵ_G is interest rate elasticity of deposit supply, $R_G(k_i, r_{-i})D_1/D$. Let k_G be the optimal level of capital. Because $\partial V_G(r_i, r_{-i}, k_i)/\partial k_i < 0$, $k_G = 0$, $\forall r_{-i}$. As the banking sector becomes perfectly competitive ($\epsilon_G \to \infty$),

$$\hat{r}(k_G) = (1 - \delta)(\alpha - \theta(\gamma - \alpha)/(1 - \theta)) + \delta\alpha < \gamma \leftarrow R_G(k_G, r_{-i}), \forall r_{-i}.$$

Therefore, if the banking sector is sufficiently competitive, the bank prefers to invest in gambling assets at the interest rate and the capital level that maximize the value from investing in gambling assets.

For the rest of the section, I assume the banking sector is sufficiently competitive so that ϵ_P and ϵ_G are sufficiently large. Because $k_G = k_P = 0$, $\hat{r}(k_P) = \hat{r}(k_G) < R_P(k_G, r_{-i}) = R_P(k_P, r_{-i})$ and hence

$$V_P(R_P(k_P, r_{-i}), r_{-i}, k_P) = V_P(R_P(k_G, r_{-i}), r_{-i}, k_G)$$
$$< V_G(R_P(k_G, r_{-i}), r_{-i}, k_G)$$
$$\leq V_G(R_G(k_G, r_{-i}), r_{-i}, k_G), \forall r_{-i}.$$

This outcome suggests that investing in gambling assets at the optimal interest rate and capital is more valuable than investing in prudent assets at the optimal interest rate and capital. As a result, investing in gambling assets without raising capital can be an equilibrium strategy.

I claim the following:

- **Equilibrium without regulation:** Suppose the banking sector is sufficiently competitive. For a symmetric equilibrium without regulation, banks invest in gambling assets and never use capital.

This pessimistic result justifies the need for regulation at least if the banking sector is sufficiently competitive. In the laissez-faire competitive economy, banks would engage in excessive risk-taking without raising capital. How can a regulator induce banks to invest in prudent assets?

To answer the preceding question, I focus on the minimum capital requirement. Notice such constraint *binds*, as banks can raise their value by reducing their capital. In order to consider capital regulation, let us start by defining a couple of key threshold interest rates. Before doing this, I define $r_P(k_i) = R_P(k_i, r_P(k_i))$ and $r_G(k_i) = R_G(k_i, r_P(k_i))$. Then, I define $\underline{k}$ and $\bar{k}$ such that

$$\underline{k} = \inf \{k_i | \hat{r}(k_i) \geq r_P(k_i)\},$$
$$\bar{k} = \inf \{k_i | \hat{r}(k_i) \geq r_G(k_i)\}.$$

I observe $\hat{r}(k_i)$ is a linear function whereas $r_P(k_i)$ and $r_G(k_i)$ are "almost" linear functions of k_i. I also observe $r_G(0) > r_P(0) > \hat{r}(0)$. $r_G(k_i)$ and $r_P(k_i)$ strictly decrease in k_i. The slope of $r_G(k_i)$ is close to $\gamma - \rho/\theta$, steeper than the slope of $r_P(k_i)$, which is close to $\alpha - \rho$. The slope of $\hat{r}(k_i)$ is strictly greater than $\alpha - \rho$, meaning that $\hat{r}(k_i)$ and $r_P(k_i)$ as well as $\hat{r}(k_i)$ and $r_G(k_i)$ intersect at a single positive point. Therefore, $\hat{r}(k_i) \geq r_P(k_i), \forall k_i \geq \underline{k}$ and $\hat{r}(k_i) \geq r_G(k_i), \forall k_i \geq \bar{k}$. In turn, $\hat{r}(k_i) < r_P(k_i), \forall k_i < \underline{k}$, and $\hat{r}(k_i) < r_G(k_i), \forall k_i < \bar{k}$.

Because $r_P(k_i)$, and $r_G(k_i)$ are almost linear in k_i with different slopes, they intersect at a single point. Let such point be $\tilde{k}$. Then, $\tilde{k}$ satisfies

$$r_p(\tilde{k}) = (\alpha(1 + \tilde{k}) - \rho\tilde{k})\frac{\epsilon_P}{\epsilon_P + 1} = (\gamma(1 + \tilde{k}) - \rho\tilde{k}/\theta)\frac{\epsilon_G}{\epsilon_G + 1} = r_G(\tilde{k}).$$

Because $\epsilon_P = \epsilon_G$ at $\tilde{k}$, $\tilde{k}$ is simplified as

$$\tilde{k} = \theta(\gamma - \alpha)/((1 - \theta)\rho - \theta(\gamma - \alpha)).$$

In turn, $\underline{k}$ is the intersection of $r_P(k_i)$ and $\hat{r}(k_i)$. Considering the slopes and intercepts of $r_P(k_i)$ and $\hat{r}(k_i)$, if $\epsilon_P/(\epsilon_P + 1)$ becomes smaller, the intersecting point also becomes smaller. Notice $\epsilon_P/(\epsilon_P + 1) < \lim_{\epsilon_P \to \infty} \epsilon_P/(\epsilon_P + 1) = 1$. Then, $\underline{k}$ is strictly less than its limit as $\epsilon_P \to \infty$. As $\epsilon_P \to \infty$,

$$\underline{k} \to \theta(\gamma - \alpha)/((1 - \theta)\rho - \theta(\gamma - \alpha)).$$

Thus,

$$\underline{k} < \theta(\gamma - \alpha)/((1 - \theta)\rho - \theta(\gamma - \alpha)) = \tilde{k}.$$

I finally consider whether $\bar{k}$ is greater than $\underline{k}$. Suppose $\underline{k} \geq \bar{k}$. Start by considering $r_P(\bar{k}) \neq r_G(\bar{k})$. From the preceding, $\hat{r}(\bar{k}) \leq r_P(\bar{k})$. Therefore,

$$V_P(r_P(\bar{k}), r_P(\bar{k}), \bar{k}) \leq V_G(r_P(\bar{k}), r_P(\bar{k}), \bar{k})$$
$$< V_G(r_G(\bar{k}), r_P(\bar{k}), \bar{k}).$$

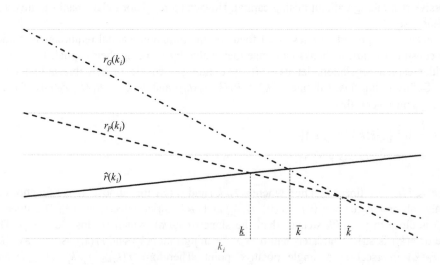

Figure 8.1 Key Functions and Thresholds for Capital Requirement

Moreover, $\hat{r}(\bar{k}) \geq r_G(\bar{k})$. Therefore,

$$V_P(r_P(\bar{k}), r_P(\bar{k}), \bar{k}) > V_P(r_G(\bar{k}), r_P(\bar{k}), \bar{k})$$
$$\geq V_G(r_G(\bar{k}), r_P(\bar{k}), \bar{k}).$$

Then, I get a contradiction. Next, consider $r_P(\bar{k}) = r_G(\bar{k})$. Then, $\bar{k} = \tilde{k} > \underline{k}$, so I get a contradiction again. Thus, $\underline{k} < \bar{k}$.

Figure 8.1 plots the key functions and thresholds for this analysis.

Let the minimum capital requirement be k^*. If $\underline{k} \leq k^* < \bar{k}$,

$$V_P(r_P(k^*), r_P(k^*), k^*) \geq V_G(r_P(k^*), r_P(k^*), k^*).$$

Then, it is also *possible* to have[2]

$$V_P(r_P(k^*), r_P(k^*), k^*) < V_G(r_G(k^*), r_P(k^*), k^*).$$

Hence, banks may prefer to gamble by setting higher interest rates. However, imposing interest rate ceiling $\bar{r}$, where $r_P(k^*) \leq \bar{r} \leq \hat{r}(k^*)$, banks are incentive-compatible with investing in prudent assets. This is because, for $\forall r_i \leq \bar{r}$ and $\forall r_{-i}$,

$$V_P(r_i, r_{-i}, k^*) \geq V_G(r_i, r_{-i}, k^*).$$

Then, banks choose to invest in prudent assets with interest rate $r_P(k^*)$. If $k^* \geq \bar{k}$,

$$V_P(r_G(k^*), r_P(k^*), k^*) \geq V_G(r_G(k^*), r_P(k^*), k^*).$$

Then, even if banks adjust interest rates for gambling, they are incentive-compatible with investing in prudent assets. If $k^* \geq \bar{k}$, a regulator does not need an interest rate ceiling in order to induce prudent investment.

In summary, I claim the following:

- **Equilibrium with regulation:** Suppose the banking sector is sufficiently competitive. There is an equilibrium in which banks invest in prudent assets with interest rate $r_P(k^*)$ under the minimum capital requirement k^* and the interest rate ceiling $\bar{r}$, where $r_p(k^*) \leq \bar{r} \leq \hat{r}(k^*)$, if $\underline{k} \leq k^* < \bar{k}$. There is an equilibrium in which banks invest in prudent assets with interest rate $r_P(k^*)$ under the minimum capital requirement k^* and no interest rate ceiling if $k^* \geq \bar{k}$.

This result suggests that a regulator can induce banks to invest in prudent assets with a moderate capital requirement and interest rate cap. If the capital requirement is severe, a regulator does not require an interest rate cap in order to induce prudent investment.

How can a regulator choose a policy? Recalling that one role of a bank is liquidity provision through deposit supply, raising banks' interest rates as high as possible is efficient as it maximizes deposit supply. Under the proposed regulation earlier, the equilibrium interest rate $r_P(k^*)$ strictly decreases in k^*. Then, minimizing k^* is desirable. From this viewpoint, it is better to set $k^* = \underline{k}$, relative to higher requirements, if the interest rate ceiling is available. If the interest rate ceiling is unavailable, it is better to set $k^* = \bar{k}$, relative to higher requirements. The other consideration is the crowding-out effect of bank capital. As the cost of capital ρ is higher than the rate of return from a prudent investment α, using capital for that prudent investment reduces relatively value-enhancing opportunities in the economy. From this viewpoint, as well as the consideration of deposit supply, minimizing capital requirement k^* is preferable.

8.5 Ongoing debate on capital regulation

Although the previous model suggests the merits of imposing capital regulation, the discussion on the effect of capital regulation has lasted a few decades but has not reached a consensus. For example, capital regulations are often criticized for their reduction of liquidity provision (Diamond and Rajan, 2000) and bank lending (Thakor, 1996), as well as the crowding out of deposits (Gorton and Winton, 2017). Moreover, recent studies suggest that banks might bypass capital regulations (e.g., Kisin and Manela, 2016). If regulatory arbitrage is possible, capital regulations might encourage banks to shift their risky lending practices into shadow banking (Plantin, 2014) or simply shift investments into risky projects within the same asset class (Duchin and Sosyura, 2014). Nevertheless, some studies suggest the necessity of capital regulation. For example, Morrison and White (2005) find that capital regulation is an efficient tool enabling regulators to combat moral hazard and enhance screening outcomes. Mehran and Thakor (2011) show both theoretically and empirically that bank values are positively correlated with equity capital.

The empirical and simulation results about the effects of capital requirements are also mixed. Opponents of capital regulation argue that it is costly for banks and society (e.g., Baker and Wurgler, 2015; Kisin and Manela, 2016; Van den Heuvel, 2008), reduces bank lending (Aiyar et al. 2014), and fails to reduce risk (Rime, 2001). Others find the effects of capital requirements are conditional. Berger and Bouwman (2009) test the relationship between capital and liquidity creation and find that it tends to be positive for large banks and negative for small ones. Others find that the effects of capital regulations depend on ownership structure (Laeven and Levine, 2009) or economic condition (Demirguc-Kunt et al., 2013).

8.6 Discussion

The capital structure of a bank is distinct from a usual firm due to its role of providing liquidity to investors. Then, a bank is subject to a *self-fulfilling* financial crisis, because a bank run indeed occurs if investors *believe* that a bank would face a liquidity shortage. A regulator resolves this problem through deposit insurance. However, insured deposits generate another problem: excessive risk-taking. Through this side effect, deposit insurance aggravates a bank's monitoring role, which is the other important role of a bank. As a remedy, a regulator can impose capital requirements to induce a prudent risk strategy. The drawback of this policy is the crowding-out effect of bank capital and the shortage of deposit supply. Still, a regulator can use interest rate control to mitigate this concern.

Although I focus on capital requirement in this section, the model of Gropp and Vesala (2001) also suggests that a bank's monitoring increases by the level of a bank's asset return. If a bank earns substantive profits, its opportunity cost of default is large, inducing a bank to increase monitoring intensity to avoid its failure. This result suggests that a bank tends to invest prudently or monitor carefully if the banking sector is concentrative because it is more profitable. On the other hand, it tends to invest aggressively or monitor less intensively if the banking sector is competitive because it is less profitable. This result is consistent with the result of Hellmann et al. (2000) that assumes the competitive banking sector to derive no-prudence equilibrium in a laissez-faire economy.

The natural question is whether reducing competition in the banking sector really improves the monitoring role of a bank. To address this question, Allen and Gale (2004) introduce the model of deposit market competition and derive Cournot equilibrium. They find that market concentration raises a bank's charter value and monitoring intensity. This is called the *margin effect*. This result is against a typical antitrust view that market competition is welfare-enhancing. They rather suggest that market competition could be inefficient for the banking sector. However, Boyd and De Nicoló (2005) focus on the loan market and find the concentration of loan suppliers (banks) raises loan rates, encouraging entrepreneurs to default. In turn, it aggravates a bank's financial stability. This is called the *risk-shifting* effect. The theoretical debate between the two parties ultimately converges to the claim by Martinez-Miera and Repullo (2010)—both effects are present.

Notes

1 As discussed later, I focus on symmetric equilibria.
2 Under our definition of $\bar{k}$, it is also possible to have

$$V_P(r_P(k^*), r_P(k^*), k^*) \geq V_G(r_G(k^*), r_P(k^*), k^*),$$

if $\underline{k} \leq k^* < \bar{k}$. In the original paper, the authors define $\bar{k}$ as the exact threshold for the preceding inequality to hold. In other words, if $\underline{k} \leq k^* < \bar{k}$, the following inequality unambiguously holds:

$$V_P(r_P(k^*), r_P(k^*), k^*) < V_G(r_G(k^*), r_P(k^*), k^*).$$

In this sense, our definition of $\bar{k}$ is more "conservative" than the one in the original paper.

Bibliography

Aiyar, S., Calomiris, C. W., Hooley, J., Korniyenko, Y., and Wieladek, T. (2014). The international transmission of bank capital requirements: Evidence from the UK. *Journal of Financial Economics*, 113(3):368–82.

Allen, F. and Gale, D. (2004). Competition and financial stability. *Journal of Money, Credit, and Banking*, 36(3):453–80.

Baker, M. and Wurgler, J. (2015). Do strict capital requirements raise the cost of capital? Bank regulation, capital structure, and the low-risk anomaly. *American Economic Review*, 105(5):315–20.

Berger, A. N. and Bouwman, C. H. (2009). Bank liquidity creation. *Review of Financial Studies*, 22 (9):3779–837.

Boyd, J. H. and De Nicoló, G. (2005). The theory of bank risk taking and competition revisited. *Journal of Finance*, 60(3):1329–43.

Bryant, J. (1980). A model of reserves, bank runs, and deposit insurance. *Journal of Banking and Finance*, 4(4):335–44.

Demirguc-Kunt, A., Detragiache, E., and Merrouche, O. (2013). Bank capital: Lessons from the financial crisis. *Journal of Money, Credit and Banking*, 45(6):1147–64.

Diamond, D. W. (1984). Financial intermediation and delegated monitoring. *Review of Economic Studies*, 51(3):393–414.

Diamond, D. and Dybvig, P. (1983). Bank runs, deposit insurance, and liquidity. *Journal of Political Economy*, 91(3):401–19.

Diamond, D. W. and Rajan, R. G. (2000). A theory of bank capital. *Journal of Finance*, 55(6):2431–65.

Duchin, R. and Sosyura, D. (2014). Safer ratios, riskier portfolios: Banks' response to government aid. *Journal of Financial Economics*, 113(1):1–28.

Gorton, G. and Winton, A. (2017). Liquidity provision, bank capital, and the macroeconomy. *Journal of Money, Credit and Banking*, 49(1):5–37.

Gropp, R. and Vesala, J. (2001). Deposit insurance and moral hazard: Does the counterfactual matter? *Working Paper 47*, European Central Bank.

Hellmann, T. F., Murdock, K. C., and Stiglitz, J. E. (2000). Liberalization, moral hazard in banking, and prudential regulation: Are capital requirements enough? *American Economic Review*, 90(1):147–65.

Kisin, R. and Manela, A. (2016). The shadow cost of bank capital requirements. *Review of Financial Studies*, 29(7):1780–820.

Laeven, L. and Levine, R. (2009). Bank governance, regulation and risk taking. *Journal of Financial Economics*, 93(2):259–75.

Martinez-Miera, D. and Repullo, R. (2010). Does competition reduce the risk of bank failure? *Review of Financial Studies*, 23(10):3638–64.

Mehran, H. and Thakor, A. (2011). Bank capital and value in the cross-section. *Review of Financial Studies*, 24(4):1019–67.

Morrison, A. D. and White, L. (2005). Crises and capital requirements in banking. *American Economic Review*, 95(5):1548–72.

Pennacchi, G. (2009). Deposit insurance, bank regulation, and financial system risks. *Journal of Monetary Economics*, 53(1):1–30.

Plantin, G. (2014). Shadow banking and bank capital regulation. *Review of Financial Studies*, 28 (1):146–75.

Rime, B. (2001). Capital requirements and bank behaviour: Empirical evidence for Switzerland. *Journal of Banking and Finance*, 25(4):789–805.

Thakor, A. V. (1996). Capital requirements, monetary policy, and aggregate bank lending: Theory and empirical evidence. *Journal of Finance*, 51(1):279–324.

Van den Heuvel, S. J. (2008). The welfare cost of bank capital requirements. *Journal of Monetary Economics*, 55(2):298–320.

INDEX

Note: Page numbers in *italics* indicate a figure and page numbers in **bold** indicate a table on the corresponding page. Note information is denoted with n and note number following the page number.

additivity 6–8, 9, 11
agency cost 2
agency problem: absence of 14; risky debt aggravating 22–3; safe debt mitigating 17–22; shirking due to 21; underinvestment due to 18–19, 22, 24–7
agency theory: on agency cost 2; on efficient level of investment 25–6; on equilibrium level of effort 20, *21*; on equilibrium level of investment 18–19, *19*, 24–6, *26*; on optimal effort under debt 21; on optimal investment under debt 19–21; overinvestment or risk shifting in 23–7, 78; overview of 2, 17, 27; payoff of stakeholders in 22–3, **23**; risky debt aggravating agency problem in 22–3; safe debt mitigating agency problem in 17–22; on shirking due to agency problem 21; on socially optimal level of effort 20, *20*; on socially optimal level of investment 17, *18*; trade-off theory versus 27; underinvestment or debt overhang in 18–19, 22, 24–7
Aghion, P. 42
Allen, F. 92
arbitrage, absence of 4, 6–9, 11, 61–2
Arrow-Debreu Model 2, 4–5, 8, 11n2, 61–3
asset tangibility 15
asymmetric information: debt as signal 55–6; overview of 2, 49, 57–8; pecking-order versus trade-off theory 2, 56–7; retained ownership as signal 51–5; underpricing in IPOs 49–51

Baker, M. 57
bank capital structure: bank run and **84**, 84–5, 92; capital regulation/requirement for 87–92, *90*; consumer types and 80–5, **82**; default and 83, 86, 87, 92; deposit insurance and 80, 84–7, 92; efficient outcome **82**, 82–5, **84**; equilibria 81, **82**, 82–4, **84**, 87–8, 91; overview of 2–3,

92; risk-taking and 85–92; shadow banking and 91; suspension of convertibility and 84–5; two roles of banks and 80, 92; unintended consequences of deposit insurance and 85–7, 92
bank run **84**, 84–5, 92
bankruptcy: bank 83, 86, 87, 92; insurance for 73; managerial loss from 55, 56; risky debt with 22–3; trade-off theory on costs of 2, 12–15, 57, 72–3
Barclay, M. J. 15
Berger, A. N. 91
Berkovitch, E. 22, 24
Black-Scholes model 64
Bolton, P. 42
boundary conditions 71–4, **72**
Bouwman, C. H. 91
Boyd, J. H. 92
Bradley, M. 12
Brownian motion 59–60
Bryant, J. 80

Calomiris, C. W. 15
capital regulation/requirement 87–92, *90*
capital structure: agency theory on 2, 17–27, 78; asymmetric information and 2, 49–58; of banks 2–3, 80–93; continuous-time model of 2, 59–79; contract theory on 2, 28–48; in frictionless capital market 2, 4–11, 61–2, 63; irrelevance or neutrality of 8–11, 63–70; overview of 1–3; security design and 2, 28–48; trade-off theory on 2, 12–16, 27, 56–7, 72–8
CARA *see* constant absolute risk aversion
CDF *see* cumulative distribution function
CDFC *see* convexity of cumulative distribution function
commitment device 47, 85

94